AS THE CHAIR TURNS...

UNTANGLING THE MEANING OF LIFE

SHELLY DEVLIN

Enjoy the Journey
Shelly

INSPYR ENTERPRISES

Dear reader:

This book is purposely printed in 14 font because 16 font is the official size of large print and ...

"WE AREN'T THERE YET FRIENDS!"

Dedicated to...
My two Josh's, the loves of my life.
May this help you understand more
how your mom/wife
is wired for sound
24/7
love you both

Part One...
THE PROCESS THAT MADE ME, its highlights and lowlights

Part two...
adding in some COLOR

Part three...
WHAT COMPLETED ME, WITH processing time AND the finishing
touches

PREFACE

Being a hairdresser is a magical career and has made me realize the power of people's stories. As the Chair Turns, first in the series, is a compilation of stories gathered from many years behind the chair. Dozens of journals saying *"someday I was going to write a book"*. A long-time labor of love began with pages and pages of bullet points, run on sentences, ellipses and has finally come to life for you the reader . These stories have impacted my life as I stood behind the chair listening to clients and watching their emotional reflection in my mirror. I have been told that I am a compassionate humble woman and I've always said everyone has a story that could make your hair curl.

I've never worn my own stories on my sleeve. I have always kept my tragic stories of being molested as a child, surviving a divorce from my high school sweetheart and walking the edge of bankruptcy to name a few neatly tucked away in my pocket. Not a secret, just not worn on my sleeve. Taking my stories out on occasion when I felt as if I received a message from the universe that it was time to share. I live to help others to find their true happy and celebrate with them while living thru life's ups and downs. There were times I did not know why I shared a story but the soulful connection I made with people was magical.

May you find a particular story that evokes a warm memory in yourself or a much-needed cry to heal. May you laugh and find yourself at home in the pages of this memoir. I'm here to INSPYR, empower and pay tribute to life and the souls that surround us. As I share my stories and peel back the layers of what has shaped me, my intent is a learning lesson for all...

To be whoever you want to be,
and to do whatever you want to do,
with the short time, we have on this planet.

ACKNOWLEDGMENTS

I am very blessed to have been a part of so many lives that have inspired me . It is truly impossible to recognize everyone. It all started with a dream and a bunch of journals.

Then I met...THE Deborah Monk. She started a writer's group to hold me accountable which turned that dream into a reality.

Then there is my writers group friend Mandra Biscornet who keeps the reality in our group and is a no-nonsense-get-shit-done kinda girl. In three years, we have grown closer together having experienced similar life tragedies.

A think tank of talented artists brainstorming together for the book cover and other book parts and pieces necessary for completing the project. Cheers to all the coffee that kept the creative juices flowing and the gasping for air when a great idea or phrase came across our lips.

To my Editor Dawn Reno Langley for insisting I actually learn the art of writing a book and talked me through many days of *"who would want to read this?"*.

My best friend Michelle always said I should write a book. She has stood by my side through all the adventures, with absolutely no judgement; truly a better friend than I.

My work wife and partner in crime through the years Sheri McCall Gayer for always believing I could do ANYTHING and do it right.

To my mom who just pops on her rose-colored glasses and stalks my adventures thru Facebook ...I have cherished every time we sit up north with coffee and slow down.

My dad who continues to be the example of hard work.

My husband who dropped out of the sky and I always joke he must be a dream and the alien ship will be back to get him soon.

Thanks to my traveling team blue for making these adventures stretch across miles.

To my son who is a talented humble beautiful soul may all your dreams come true.

My hairdressing coworkers who have influenced my life since the first day I stepped foot in a salon when I was 18.

To all the clients that I have had the true honor of sharing a piece of your life, even if it was for 30 minutes every 6 weeks. Thank you

PART I
THE PROCESS THAT MADE ME...

IT'S HIGHLIGHTS AND LOWLIGHTS

The process of life takes time. Through the twists and turns, I learned life is about perception, positive vs. negative. I gained knowledge through life's experiences while I aged with infinite wisdom. Everyone has a story that could make your hair curl. The difference is how you end that chapter, is it victory or defeat? Is it sorrow or joy? Is it pride or shame?

Learn the rules like a master,
then break them
and become an artist
∼A twist on the words of Pablo Picasso

CHAPTER 1

My Passion

Two-thirds of my life has been spent behind the chair at The Water's Edge Salon and Spa, the love of my life, the corporation I nurtured for close to three decades and four locations. The other third included; house-call hairdresser for home-bound elders, salon owner (mom to all), on set hairstylist-artist-sculptor, trade show platform entertainer, but all of my hats revolved around being a hairdresser. In reality, however, I was also a daughter, wife, mom, sister, niece, cousin and a friend to many.

The days in the salon were always a new adventure. The

clients and I laughed about silly things, like the time my client Jackie decided to give her husband a haircut at home only a few hours before his new job interview. Rushing around the house with her typical red-flushed-face, and kids underfoot, she forgot to add the guard to the clippers. As she held the rattling, needing-to-be-oiled set of men's grooming clippers, she zipped a clean-cut, bald, racing stripe right up the back of his head. She stood in disbelief for a moment, then went into action like a woman on a mission.

She told her husband to get in the car. She drove him directly to my salon and stormed in the front door like a boss, exclaiming, "Bob has a job interview. I need you to fix this!"

Clients always thought I had a magic wand mixed in with my combs and brushes.

"Well," I said, looking at Bob with a grin, "it's been a long time since the military, but a bald fade is going to look crisp and in control for your interview. The alternative is a black sharpie, coloring in what your wife has done to the back of your head." We all chuckled and chose the military haircut.

Clients have showed me everything from their boudoir photo shoots, to how good their breast implants were healing, to pics of their fetishes (some of which I wish I could un-see). Although I feel grateful to be their confidant, I have created a no judgement zone, a safe haven for them to share. But selfies of leather harnesses with a giant rubber penis attached to it makes me stutter and search for what to say. Ohhhh, th...ats beau...t..i..ful? or Great out...fit!

Some were young enough to warrant a booster-seat in order to get their first haircuts and some have been old enough for adult diapers. Sometimes our first meeting meant I would be doing their hair for their wedding and someday cutting the hair of their babies. Others built a relationship with me later in life, and I held their hand till the very end, literally.

Yes, that's me. A Hairdresser. If I was lucky, I got to be their hero, their friend, their confidant. I felt like an important person in their lives. Invited to parties, showered with gifts, a person they told their trials and tribulations to. They shared their successes, failures and rattled on for days as if we were long lost friends. They visited the salon just because, often when they didn't even have an appointment. I have heard them come in the front door, pause, breath out a relaxing sigh and say, 'aahhh I'm home"

I love the kids: so sweet, so innocent, with wonderful lives ahead of them. I remember one adorable, curly-haired boy who asked his mom to invite his friend, his hairdresser Shelly, to his third birthday party. It touches my heart to now see him grown, married and having babies of his own.

Tia, a teenaged girl tasked with writing a school paper about a great American woman of history, asked her teacher if she could write about me. I have that A+ essay hanging in my office. Seeing Tia grow to a beautiful woman and an amazing mom makes me feel as if I have magic that surrounds me.

Tommy was three when I first cut his hair. He had chosen

to be silent, that little soul spoke to no one but his parents. At age six, he spoke for the first time, and I was one of the very few he chose to speak to. I never treated him differently, always sat him in the chair and would say "how would you like your hair today Tommy?' I didn't want him to feel uncomfortable so I never made eye contact and then I'd hear his mother answer for him. That day was no different from all the others until a different voice answered me, a voice of a little boy, "A little shorter please". I turned away with an elated smile and glanced at his mom and dad with a tear in my eye. I've known him from booster-seat age to over six feet tall and becoming a genuinely wonderful humble human being! What an amazing kid.

The clients and I have cried over death, divorce and disease. Deaths that ranged from infants to elders and all ages in between. Death by their own hand or from a disease that took them too young. Divorces that were civil and ones that tore lives apart, including one where the couple fought about who got to keep the hairdresser. (But that's another story for another day.)

Other days, I take the stage: heels on, rhinestone necklace, and spotlight on me. Onstage, my chair holds a beautiful model as I teach about product, patience and practice to an audience ranging from 10 to 10,000. My inspiration flows through my fingertips to show technique, and I share inspirational stories with hairdressers ranging in age from 15 to 98.

At one point, I was presented with a pin from a local cosmetology school in Chicago, Illinois, thanking me for years of inspiration for their young students attending the show. It was a must stop in their field trip itinerary at the Aquage stage to see me do my magic.

A crying salon owner came to the edge of my stage after one presentation to say that after hearing my story of being burned by employees a few times during my career as a salon owner, she was confident she would survive. She sobbed as she held my hand, took a deep breath and said, "Thank you."

My crowning moment was seeing my favorite little lady come to the edge of my stage year after year. Years in, I found out her name: Margaret. She wheeled up in her wheelchair in her coiffed hairdo with a radiant smile, and she would clap uncontrollably as if she was a child at a magic show. Always dressed impeccably, that woman was Margaret Vinci Heldt who invented the 'beehive' doo in 1960 for the front cover of *Modern Salon* magazine. On March 23, 2016, she wheeled to the front of my stage one last time at the age of 98 and sadly passed away 4 months later. I will cherish July's 2016 issue of Modern Salon magazine as they paid tribute to her on page 36, while my work graced the front cover and pages in between. What an honor for the two of us to be featured that month in a beautiful trade magazine.

Throughout the years, I have always listened intently, and on occasion, cautiously gave advice. I always wanted to believe I could help my clients in some way, but many times I had to learn to protect myself from the emotional vampires, the whiners, the half-empty-life-sucking-pity-partiers. I learned fast they could steal my mojo and empty my inspiration tank instantly. But I cannot waste words on some of that craziness.

House calls for my elders was another passion. I could sit and listen to their stories of "back in the day" for hours! Mama Lou and Anna Banana were two house-bound ladies, their nicknames given lovingly by their daughters, with whom they lived. Anna Banana, a sweet but stern Italian woman from Medford, Massachusetts, and her roommate Mama Lou a petite, adorable British woman who literally spoke as if she was a live Hallmark card.

Anna wanted to know more about me than to share stories about herself. But one day after her haircut, she took my hand and led me down the hallway to show me something. Her family portrait. We stood in front of an elegantly-framed, 16x20 family heirloom. Anna stood about four feet eight and leaned against the foot of the bed. She spoke stern and confidant like she was a museum historian. Her voice was slow and steady, as she told me the picture was taken in 1929, when she was five years old. The sepia tones softened the photograph that was in pristine condition. She told me the story of her father being a custom tailor for Harvard Coop in the 1920's in Medford, Massachusetts.

Mama Lou had two favorites in life: cats and her family.

As I brushed through her hair she would close her eyes and say, "if I was a cat I would be purring right now," and she kept her eyes closed, drifting off into a daydream. When I would prompt her with questions, her eyes would snap open and she'd start her stories as if I dropped a quarter into an old fortune telling machine.

"This is a beautiful silver tea set," I said one day. "Tell me about it." I never imagined she would tell me the story of her father being the silversmith for the Titanic!

My hair life has no boundaries. I eat and drink salon life. It intertwines in my soul. The remnants of a hairdresser never wash's off. I live it, breath it. It's in my blood and my soul. It travels home with me.

My baby brother (17 years younger) once questioned what the fluffy pink stuff in the deli case at Shaw's grocery store was. He sat curiously with his legs dangling from the grocery cart in his Ninja Turtles t-shirt.

"Mousse," I told him. He held out his three-year-old hand as if he was holding a pile of that fluffy pink mousse and pretended to work it into his hair. With a confused look on his face, he said "MOUSSE?" I realized the only mousse he knew about (due to his hairdresser sister) was mousse as a hair product ...not the tasty dessert.

My own son at the same delicate age of three, knew the difference between blue and teal and referred to yellow as blonde, truly a hairdresser's kid. But the all-time best is picking my son up from 5th grade and having him be in full disgust and disbelief about the new girl in school. He said, "Mom, you should have seen the size of her mustache! Why doesn't her mom take her to the salon to have it waxed off?"

I am a hairdresser, through and through.

MENOPAUSE IN PROGRESS...
go around me, and do not make eye contact!
Warning: Due to the influence of hormones,
I could Burst into tears or kill you in the next 5 minutes
~Unknown

CHAPTER 2

Coming Apart at the Seams

It's Tuesday night at 9 pm and the staff has punched out, literally and figuratively. I look around: magazines left askew, a few rogue hair balls litter the floor, 15 lights left on, and I start going through the salon check list of closing items. Apparently, a checkmark with a pen doesn't mean you have actually completed the task. My blood pressure rises, yet I continue wiping down counters, start a load of laundry and make a list for tomorrow. At almost 50 years old I guess your patience starts to fade.

I always start the day put together with glamour and glitz, but glamour and glitz clocked out with the staff. I plop down in the hair chair to take a breath, and I wish "I" could just clock out! My purple eyeshadow is replacing my blush, my rose blush has now slid to my jaw line, and my blue cosmic lipstick has melted into the crease in my neck. As I spin the chair to face the full-length mirror, my sweaty and defeated reflection stares back at me. My feet are throbbing, my shoulders are burning and there is nothing fresh about me. If the floors were tile, I'd lay my tired body flat out onto the cold, hard floor and press my sweaty face against it. I muster up one last surge of energy and spin the chair, close my eyes, and take another deep breath. I'm hoping my magic chair will act like a time machine and fast forward me through the end of the night to-do's and teleport me safely to my comfy warm bed.

A meandering thought pops into my brain, and I can remember being ten years old when inspired thoughts flooded my attention and tugged on my creative mind. My dreams dodging back and forth between owning my own shiny Peterbilt big rig with a sleeper cab traveling cross country or, being an eccentric interior designer, designing million-dollar homes for the stars. Those dreams disappeared and later in high school, I saw myself living in New York City working for a graphic design company, or even becoming a counselor, a psychologist to help with people's problems. What a wide array of paths to follow. I may not have ever been sure of what path to take but I always felt like there were bread crumbs placed on my path to direct my way.

Little did I know, but I have followed the bread crumbs to the perfect career. Being a hairdresser embodies the art and adventure I dreamed of when I was young. My career brings me to exotic places, where I have met talented people doing amazing things. Hairdressers are unique artists building sculptures using hair as their medium. And like a counselor, I listen to the souls in my chair, I listen to their problems and personal journeys. Their inspired and sensational experiences have changed and carved their lives, listening to them also changes and carves my life.

A quick snap of my magic-filled cape, and it's laid across the shoulders of my next client. That person is never just a client to me; they are friends, mentors, and family. No matter who it is, I'm ready to let the inspiration flow, while making them beautiful on the outside and healed on the inside.

This career, this way of life I've chosen for myself, brings me full circle into peoples lives. From the conception of birth to the bitter end in death, through tough times and best of times I hold their hand while making them beautiful. I'm privy to my client's deepest and darkest secrets and fears, their loves, their hates, their job changes, family trysts and lusty affairs. Having the honor of holding many a hand through sickness and physical challenges, beautifying their balding, chemo-riddled heads and spirits like a secret fairy on their shoulder, I whisper strength in their ears. I become their trusted friend when they need one. I adore my clients and I wonder sometimes, who rescued who? Surrounding my chair is a powerful galaxy of human interaction and life experiences resulting in laughter, tears and profound soul lessons.

Jolted back to reality as if I was in the Back to The Future car, I open my eyes. My life, my mission, my passion, just played out in my head in an intense daydream. My soul lights up my heart with glowing strength and my body tries desperately to follow the lead!

It's been a long day standing behind the chair. I lock up, climb into the truck and head a mile down the street to a friend's massage office where I treat myself to a well-deserved massage. My soul knows passion, but it is tired, worn down and feeling beaten. I unclasp the rhinestones, peel off the sweaty leather skirt and jump into a hot shower. I wash off the day feeling fresh yet still exhausted, and climb under the warm soft sheets of the massage table.

As I lie on the massage table, I envision each thought floating up in a puff of smoke until it disintegrates. Slowly the thoughts evaporate in my mind, the list of to-dos', undone laundry, closets that need cleaning, books to read, policies to write. The hairdresser, salon owner and Shelly finally let go and drift off.

But one thought fights its way to the front, *mmm, Mexico!* I love Mexico. I can feel the heat of the sun and the sand in my toes. I spend my day reading books, lying on the beach, gazing at the turquoise waters, getting massages, and writing my next book! It's not only a great vacation plan, but it's also my retirement dream.

As my body releases, my brain taunts me with a new thought. I drift off even more in the massage; my mind, body and spirit are becoming renewed. I have been in this career for more than half of my life. I have loved it, but I am tired. No regrets or resentment. It's just time to move on. I will sell my home, my business and move to Mexico to enjoy the next 50 years. Celebrate my 100th birthday chilling by the beautiful waters of the Gulf of Mexico!

I'm in a fog after an hour, and I roll off the massage table, stretch my arms to the ceiling, stand up tall on my feet and like a bat has just struck me from behind, I say out loud, *"WHAT? Have I lost my mind? Shit! Menopause has kidnapped my brain!"* I think I must need medical attention; maybe I should call a doctor. I think I must be losing my mind! Did I just plan to move to Mexico?

Over the last few months, I've felt like something is terribly wrong. I'm coming apart at the seams. No patience for anyone these days; the world seems to be filled with fucktards! It's like there's a devil on my shoulder but she's dressed as an angel. She is so convincing putting these thoughts into my head as she says, "Sell the house, sell the business and move to Mexico!"

I say to the devil dressed as an angel, "Wait! My Mom and Dad will never fly to Mexico. I'll miss them! Wait, I thought I was supposed to help cut tomatoes in my son's new dream restaurant? What about my travel teaching job? My successful business I have built for over 25 years?"

Sanity kicks in for one minute and I come to my senses. It's clear again: I need to make my world MEXICO!

Sell the house. The house that took me out of a tough spot, the first midlife crisis. That chapter is over! My soul mate and I need a home to call ours, not the house with a few years of baggage that was mine.

Sell the business! Or close the doors, call it Chapter 27, as in, 27 years in business; no that will quickly turn into Chapter 13 in the small-town gossip page of Facebook. Call it Plan B(I chuckle) that Plan B is the morning after pill! Like it could be life's "do-over" pill! Scrap both plans. Journal out: Plan C, D, E, F, along with plan WTF! Ok, soul search, gather strength, breathe!

I think menopause is officially trying to kick my ass! I have only taken a happy pill once in my life, one prescription, one anti-depressant during the year of divorce, travel and near bankruptcy but that's another book or chapter! The thought of not being strong enough to handle life has reared its ugly head again! In my head I hear, give my baby (the salon I've nurtured for over 25 years) up for adoption to the best mom I know. Selling the business is like taking your bra off after a long day. You feel an incredible relief from being so bound. I want to feel that relief. I want less responsibility. I want to be the big sister, not the mom.

The doctor asked, "Do you have any added stress?"

"Really? You have to ask that?" I answered. "I don't know. Is its normal stress to be selling a house, buying a house, contemplating selling a business after 25 years, and dealing with your mom's cancer diagnosis and your dog dying?"

"Seems like normal everyday life, but I definitely don't

have an edge, I definitely don't have a leg up." My voice cracks, the flood gates open and I continue. "And I definitely don't have a fuse that is very long at all."

I clench my blue paper doctor's office gown, sobbing. "When you wake up in the morning and the first thing that's on your mind is the dreaded to-do list that inevitably seems like it'll take three weeks to get done, and you only have eight hours to make it happen, there's a heaviness that makes you want to pull the blankets back over your head and ignore the world, snuggle up with the dogs and just flee from reality! Go back to sleep, close the door, don't answer the phone!"

I gasp for another breath. "The only thing that feels stable is your soulmate lying next to you and your dog lying by your feet. Everything else is like a giant black spinning tornado!"

The doctor's eyes fill with tears, and I'm trying to analyze whether she is sympathetic or about to call the white coats! She calmly writes me a prescription. "It'll take about two weeks for the medication to take effect," she gingerly tells me.

I wish I had an emergency life shut-off that I could pull and give myself two weeks to balance out my crazy brain and stop this tornado inside my soul. God give me strength! Why can't I just juggle life like I used to? Turning 50 is a bitch! I'm not afraid of the actual number; it's the emotional rollercoaster of aches, pains and emotions that gets to me.

Enter a little Prozac. I wonder if you'll always remember the day that you start your first prescription of Prozac. It's like a life event similar to when your kid loses his first tooth or shaves his mustache for the first time. This little pill is only going to mask, cover, Novocain the systems of pre-menopause, menopause, getting old or whatever it is that the medical doctors are calling it.

I make a second call to a therapy office. This young-not-old-enough to have any problems girl answers the phone. "I'll need to ask you a few questions to best fit you to a therapist," she tells me.

"Let me sum this up for you," I say sternly. "I need a woman over 50 who has been through menopause, divorce, children, as well as financial success and despair. That's who I need."

Enter Doctor Pat, my official life coach. She is like my long-lost big sister and her words come out like warm hugs. Her spirit is strong like coffee, and she sorted out my thoughts and gave me valuable advice.

"When you get in your head, get out! Say it out loud," she'd say.

We laughed, cried, and chuckled through sorting out life's stressors. Although Doctor Pat didn't have a cure, she felt like a fellow crusader helping a broken woman down the bumpy treacherous road of aging and life.

Tuesday morning is the salon world's Monday. I unlocked the front door, and I stepped into the beautiful building of The Water's Edge Salon and Spa, I could feel the inspiration! I looked at the bright blue walls of the charming 1827 home as I walked through. There hung the beautifully-framed front covers to Modern Salon magazine, Hot Hair magazine and Canadian Hair Magazine. That was me. I did the hair for those covers. I passed the framed licenses of all the talented staff, 'my kids', the artists I have taught to better their craft. I glance at the appointment book seeing dozens of names of clients scheduled for their Water's Edge special time. I see names of third generation clients and recall phone numbers of clients that have been coming for so long that that phone number rang to a rotary dial phone on their kitchen wall. The self-worth, the bravery, love, compassion and perseverance that I have learned from them overwhelms me. I sit down in the hair chair, the love in this place fills my heart and I look up to see a framed quote from Elizabeth Taylor:

"You just do it.

You force yourself to get up.

You force yourself to put one foot in front of the other

and goddam it you refuse to let it get to you, you fight, you cry, you curse.

Then you go about your business of living.

That's how I've done it, there is no other way."

Now, coffee in hand, I stand with hot rollers in my purple hair, an enormous rhinestone necklace around my neck, thigh high boots and rocking a mini skirt. Yes, a leather mini skirt, though I'm days away from being FIFTY! I'm ready for another day in my life as a hairdresser.

Every great dream begins with a dreamer.
Always remember,
you have within you
the strength,
the patience,
and the passion
to reach for the stars to change the world.
~Harriet Tubman

CHAPTER 3

Chock Full of Nuts

ONE SUNDAY MORNING IN SEPTEMBER, 1989, I was out in the flower gardens weeding and dreaming about opening my own salon. I was 22 and had been a hairdresser for five years. I owned a house with an unfinished walk out basement, facing a beautiful brook and flourishing flower gardens. I wanted a little place to make people pretty, on the inside and out. In the past five years, I had learned how valuable being a hairdresser really is. It's not just a flawless haircut, a perfect color, or the best braid. I started learning how extremely important a hairdresser can truly be in someone's life. The two salons I had worked in cultivating my career were worlds apart. I started piecing together what my salon would look like. Sharing ideas with family and friends.

I would wander down to my basement. This house used to be my grandparents and it came with all their stuff. I'd pull the chain from the ceiling on each light bulb in the basement. Through the yellow glow I glanced around at the work benches covered with recycled peanut butter jars filled with nuts, bolts and screws. It was dusty and cluttered mostly with things my grandfather should have thrown out long ago. I could see how cute this place would be, I saw thru the clutter, the dust, the dirt, the empty boxes, and stacked newspapers. The insistent urge to open my own salon had been brewing for the past three years and this little space of three hundred square feet is going to be just perfect, I thought!

I built my career in an upscale salon nestled between a furrier and a bank in a quaint strip mall near the affluent town of Amherst, New Hampshire.

At twenty years old I now had two years' experience. I was given the opportunity to start working in a tiny Steel Magnolias-type Beauty Shoppe called Dolly's Beauty Shoppe in the rural town of Windham, New Hampshire. The sweet deal included taking over the entire property. It would be my first home with a beautiful yard, a pool, and my very own salon to make people look pretty. So, I did the responsible thing and gave a one-month notice to my upscale salon an hour away from where I was living and took the up-and-coming beauty shoppe opportunity.

I was excited for my new journey. I hand-selected Christmas cards to give to my clients and started collecting addresses. I wanted to thank them for starting my career off with such a warm welcoming. I wanted to say good bye and leave on a good note with a proper, handwritten card.

My stern Korean boss thought otherwise, and let me go two weeks into my month-long notice. Apparently angry, she didn't approve of me collecting addresses and what she thought was soliciting business. I never had any intention nor did I dream for one second that the clients would follow me. I was just a twenty-year-old kid following a dream.

I sent out my cards, and 60% of my clients show up on the steps of Dolly's Beauty Shoppe! Wow, worlds collide and these well-to-do clients are stunned and bewildered. They are now getting their hair done in a back-in-time old school beauty Shoppe, but they have faith. They wait patiently for me to transform this beauty Shoppe until it is a scene out of Cinderella getting ready for the ball.

This is where I saw a different side of the beauty industry. Sweet old ladies with weekly sets and stories to tell, mixed in with the trendy Amherst housewives, their Coach shoes and sleek blowouts. I cleaned the dusty beauty shoppe dreaming about what I would do when it was mine.

Dolly and I had fun and something magical happened. I renewed her energy, and she set retirement on a shelf. She smoked her Pall Malls and taught me how to tease out a set. I enjoyed the stories of the townies, and I brought young life and energy to Dolly's, a shoppe once filled with AARP magazines, old school perm techniques, and cap frost highlights. I started to learn and to feel the magic of being intertwined with these clients' lives. I wasn't just the hairdresser making them pretty; it was becoming much more emotional. But still, it was not my own. The thoughts of my own place weighed heavy on me, I was ready.

I imagined a magical place with flourishing colorful gardens as you entered and beautiful, bright, creative displays of products. It would be a place where people felt needed, wanted and appreciated. Tossing around potential names: Shelly's place, no, felt too much like a local bar. Beaver Brook Hair Studio...no, that would be a joke (although my house sat on the edge of the calm waters of Beaver Brook). The Water's Edge Salon...aaahhhh, yes, that made me feel peaceful yet classy! This will be no kitchen sink beauty shop, this will be a salon in my home like no other.

Dad pulled into the driveway in his dusty blue Chevy pickup that served as his office for part of the day while a bulldozer or dump truck served as his office for the rest of the time. He propped his hardworking, tanned-as-leather arm on the window, his long-sleeved Dickie uniform rolled up to his elbow. He was headed to his next job. Since Dad had owned his own business for umpteen years, I figured I'd roll the dice and ask for his advice. Picking his brain was always a crap shoot: you never knew if he was going to say anything.

Dad, aka Archie Bunker, is a man who doesn't usually speak in full sentences. He owns his own successful excavation construction company, works seven days a week, smoked three packs of Marlboros a day and drank a few Budweisers every night. His eyes are deep blue and he always has your back. He's more of a grunt, groan and nod kind of guy, a man who wears a brown Dickies outfit every day, spring, summer, fall and winter. Five days saved for special occasions when my mom pulls out his special occasion black Dickies.

When he sat in my hair chair, he always sat hesitantly, not comfortable with anyone having the upper hand but himself. He smelled of hard work and peppermint gum. He always liked the cape tight enough to not let any hair escape down his neck but joked it was too tight. No fluff and puff, no conversation. Just cut the hair and back to work. And don't try to get fancy on trimming the eyebrows and nose hair.

So today, here he sat with his arm propped on his pickup window and his nose hairs out for display like they were prize-winning walrus tusks.

"Dad, I would like to build a salon in my house."

Silence for thirty seconds, which felt like an eternity, then he asked, "When?"

"Soon," I said

"What, did you plant a tree that's sprouting thousand-dollar bills?"

There is that prize winning personality! I thought, but I held my tongue and instead, replied, "I've got a little saved but probably not enough,"

Silence again. I waited. He'll either say something or nothing.

"How much?"

"Well, I've done some researching and I think I can do the remodel and fit up for about ten thousand dollars."

Another pause, "Meet me at the house on Wednesday."

He puts his pickup in reverse, nods his chin, and drives off. I stood there, rake in hand and a smile on my face.

Wednesday rolled around, and after dinner, I headed over to my parents' house, a modest ranch that they have lived in since I was a baby. I sat across from Dad at the beautiful clawfoot antique oak dining room table that once belonged to my grandparents. I remember oiling that table as a kid as part of my chores. I walked in and Dad was sitting in "his chair."

If we were all sitting around the table and Dad came home, it was a given, without a thought, without a word, we would continue our conversation while someone would shift left or right so "his chair" was available.

I sat down across from him, with no idea what he was going to say. I was careful not to put my elbows on the table, because he didn't like that. I waited for him to speak. I felt like some profound business advice, some secret to success, was about to be unveiled. Then he grinned, the look we don't see very often, a James Dean kind of smirk. And I knew he was up to something.

"I'll be right back," he said.

He headed down to his dusty, cluttered, some-might-call-it-a-hoarder-basement. I had no idea what he was doing but he obviously thought he was being clever. I wasn't sure what silly joke he had up his sleeve. A few minutes later, he came back up the creaky wooden stairs with a bigger grin than before. In his hands, he held a Chock-Full o'-Nuts coffee can. He slid the coffee can across the table, and I peeled back the yellow plastic lid. Inside were neat little folds of money that smelled of coffee and dirt. Little packs of money in different thicknesses like they had been squirreled away for a rainy day or for a daughter who wanted to start a business. I unfolded all the packs and sorted out the tens, twenties, fifties and hundreds, making stacks on the oak table. As the stacks got higher, finally the very last bill was sorted and laid out on the table. In amazement, I yelled into the living room, "Hey, Mum", do you know how much money is here?" Her eyes never left the television and she replied, "Nope." Mom had served up hotdogs and boiled potatoes for years and there was a coffee can full of money in the basement? The grand total is $9,900 dollars. Dad flashed his James Dean grin and said, "You needed ten thousand, right?" He reached into his left shirt pocket and added a crisp one-hundred-dollar bill to the pile, the exact amount I needed to start my salon.

I will never look at a Chock-Full o' Nuts coffee can again without a grin. To me, the can is a shiny gold Genie lamp straight out of Aladdin granting me my wish. To everyone else, it's just a coffee can but I now saw the magic.

*"Never be ashamed of a scar,
It simply means you were stronger
than what tried
to hurt you"*
~Unknown

CHAPTER 4

Before the Dreams, came Nightmares

MY NEXT CLIENT shamefully walked across the old hardwood floors towards me. I had never met this kid. She wore a thick, baggy, gray hoodie, and appeared to be old enough to be a sixth grader, maybe 11 years old. No smiles from her, in fact, she almost cowered as she sat down in my chair.

Her name was Emily, shoulders hunched and her mousy brown hair hung over her eyes. She could barely see. I gently rested my hands on her shoulders and eased the hoodie from her head. When I pulled back that hoodie, the energy was ripped from my body. That hoodie unveiled horror: the front of her hair hung past her nose, the sides reached her chest, and in the back, the hair should've stretched to the middle of her back, but instead, it was matted into a tight, unkempt ball. It obviously hadn't been brushed in weeks.

This is the hair I see on clients who have spent an intolerable amount of time in the hospital, lying on their back, unable to move, and their first trip back to reality is to see me, the hairdresser. They visit my salon, sit in my chair, determined to look and feel better, almost better than any doctor could make them feel. Was this child in the hospital recently?

Her Mom, who has been standing way too close with a scowl on her face, leaned in, hovering over her daughter.

"See... see... I told you to brush your hair," she growled. "Now she's going to have to shave your head!"

That little girl, that sixth grader, shrunk even further into my chair, withdrawing into her shell like a box turtle.

I told the Mom, "I'm not going to shave her head, but this may take a few more minutes, so how about you wait in the waiting area?" I led her by her arm out of the room.

This poor young girl, still cowering in my chair, looked up through her eyelashes and through her chest-length dirty hair. I put my hands on her shoulders and cheerfully said, "Okay, friend, let's make you look even more beautiful than you are already." Silently, our eyes met, and I hope I conveyed that she was safe, right at that moment, she was okay.

My heart sank.

She was not your usual preteen who simply had poor hygiene. She was different. This was neglect. I took a deep breath, then poured all the patience and strength and love I had into my fingertips, and I gingerly combed out the unimaginable ball of tangled hair on the back of Emily's head. While I worked, I talked, hoping she would join in.

We talked about how to use shampoo, conditioner and combs. We talked about school, her pets and friends. We talked about her dream of becoming a vet, and slowly her face softened, and her shoulders relaxed. I could see the little girl emerge as she told me about herself.

An hour and a half of combing out her hair, we were ready to cut a beautiful shoulder-length layer to make her look pretty. Feeling good about how she looked would become the first piece of armor she could use to survive this world she was put into.

I whipped off The Magic Cape and turned her around. She looked into the mirror and a smile burst spontaneously across her face. It filled me with warmth.

Her Mom came back in and leered by our side. Emily's eyes locked with mine, she didn't even feel the negative energy her mom was exuding. I felt as if my magic cape shielded her.

I reviewed all of my instructions in a fun-filled tone of voice: how to shampoo, how to condition, how to care for her hair at home. I gave Emily a comb and a travel size shampoo and conditioner. "This is my card," I said, "with my number, so if you forget how to use these products, call me anytime." I could feel we both knew I meant more than that, yet still, I repeated, "You can call me anytime."

She walked out with her shoulders back and her head high, a moment of renewed strength. I wished I could've done more. A deep sense of pain engulfed me, and I wondered how long this moment of respect she had today would last?

One afternoon in August when the salon was quiet, I got word through the small world gossip grapevine that Dick the child molester had died. I had truly wanted him to live forever, in the hopes that some piece of his mind would finally realize what he'd done wrong! I wanted him to wake up at night with a ripping knot in his stomach and the look of pain in his face as his actions haunted him! I wanted him to live like he was drowning in the fiery pits of Hell, worse than the Hell he'd put others through. It's still hard to believe how incredibly fucked up your brain has to be to be a child molester.

I was in 6th grade, quiet, shy and timid, my long brown hair parted down the middle. I walked down the Windham

Center School hallway, the heels of my Dr Scholl's snapping against the polished hardwood floor. It felt as though the hallway got longer as I took each step to the counselor's office. No one else was in the halls except me, which made it even scarier.

The hand-written note in my hand was damp with sweat. As the cold metal doorknob slid in my sweaty hand, I pushed it open and stepped into Ms. Jane's office and handed her the note I had written after looking up words in the dictionary.

It read: "I'm not sure what it's called, but I looked it up in the dictionary, I think this is what's happening to me... statutory rape...sexual intercourse with a minor."

My heart was beating fast, and I remember being really warm. She read it, and looked down at me, and said, "Okay, Shelly, is this something you want me to call your parents on?"

She had no look of concern. Maybe I was wrong. Maybe I looked up the wrong word. I was just a 10-year-old kid, what did I know?

"No, that's okay." I barely found the strength to speak. Convinced I had done something wrong, I turned and walked out the door, down that long echoing hallway that now seemed darker than before.

We never spoke of it again.

Through the years, the secret kept trying to come out of the closet I'd locked it in. This time, I was a junior in high school at Pinkerton Academy. My cousin, who had lived in "his" home, was a senior in high school and had begun planning her life with her new boyfriend. She confided in him the horror of what had happened to her through the years as a child. My cousin and her boyfriend spoke to me at school one day and devised a plan that we go to the police.

I was 16.

Though it felt right to be going to the police, it was also surreal. I'd kept this a secret. The 6th grade counselor hadn't been horrified, shocked, or stunned. She was emotionless. What would be different this time? This secret had been in the closet for 6 years, but maybe there was still time to press charges. I felt deep down there had to be some kind of justice.

We went to the police station, and as we walked in, I flashed back to the time in sixth grade. The hallways of the police station felt like the hallway I'd walked down so long ago, but even though the hall was as hollow and echoing now, it feels brighter and the feeling of authority radiated as surely as if someone had arrived in a superhero cape. People there were doing the right thing. My cousin and I were separated into two rooms while her boyfriend waited in the lobby.

But it was the same as the counselor's office. The uniformed officers were emotionless, neutral, I sat in a bright white room by myself at a table and was asked to write in detail what had allegedly happened to me. I was left alone.

Writing it down was tougher than I imagined. I had lived the last six years hiding from that flashback. Whenever I felt myself going down that rabbit hole, I'd close my eyes as tight as

I could to make that scene in my head go away. As I'm writing this, I remember it felt as if I'd entered a teleporter to go hurtling back in time. I always avoided going there, to that dark place, because it was the last place on earth I wanted to visit.

The memories pummeled me, and I realized something. I tried to tape-record him one time. He must have been threatening me. Why else would I set up a cassette recorder? Trauma affects our memories, and my memories had been turned into a silent motion picture. But no, the cassette tape just revealed mumbling. No clear words. Nothing incriminating.

It played in my head, that silent movie. All the actions, but none of the words. It was hard not to close my eyes tight and make it go away, but I talked to myself, reminding my quiet little ten-year-old self that I needed to be strong.

Write it down Shelly... write it down.

Writing words on paper seemed easy until the words said "his penis." I found myself squeezing my eyes closed and squishing up my face to make the thought go away. *It's just words on paper, Shelly*, I told myself. *Write it down and this can be over.* The pen's ink appeared so dark, bold, and real.

When I finished, I put the pen down and wiped away a tear. I really felt an end in sight; finally, someone would listen and take action. Police are always supposed to do the right thing. I felt my ordeal was finally at an end, and he would get what he deserved: he would go to jail. We left the police station, and I felt a little numb, but it wasn't over. Now I had to go home and tell my parents.

Dad was at work when I got home, but Mom knew I needed to talk by the look on my face. I was pale, scared, exhausted and full of fear.

"I filled out a police report today after school," I told her. "It was about something bad that happened a long time ago. Mom, can you remember the time I called you to come pick me up at Aunt Pat's house? It was late, but I didn't want to stay there."

A shadow passed over her eyes, and I will never forget the silence in the room. Mom possesses the biggest rose-colored glasses in the world, and she couldn't imagine an event important enough for me to file a police report. There was no disbelief in her eyes, just heavy sadness. I told her how I tried to tell a counselor in sixth grade, and how sad I was for my cousin who lived in that house. I couldn't imagine how many times bad things had happened to her.

Mom didn't cry. She just had a look of pain and concern. I don't think she could let herself process what I was telling her. Someone once told me it was a "Band-Aid Face," the look of pain on someone's face when they wish they could take all the bad away. Mom had a Band-Aid face and now she knew she had to tell my dad.

It was late that night when Dad came home. I was on the top bunk in my room. Dad came in, still dressed in his work clothes and put his hand on my arm. He stood on the side of my bed in the dark, and I'm glad it was dark.

I will never forget his words: "I wish you hadn't gone to the police." I knew clearly what he meant. He somehow knew the justice system would not come through for me. He wanted to take justice into his own hands.

The next morning, we got a call from the prosecutor. What was supposed to be a judge's chambers meeting with two young innocent girls to push the charges through and sentence him, turned into a trial with a jury. I pictured the old Perry Mason show. I'd have to be on the stand being questioned by the defense attorney.

I screamed, "I can't do that! I can barely recall this silent horror movie and put it down on paper! I have to actually openly talk out loud about it? And be questioned?"

My secret had crumbled, again back in the closet it went.

The secret closet opened again on Easter Sunday when I was 25 years old. My husband and I went to his mother's apartment complex, my husband was in front of me as we climbed the stairs.

He opened the door, said hello as he peeked his head in, then abruptly shut the door. In the dark staircase, he looked down at me in complete disbelief, as if he had seen a ghost.

"Dick the child molester is sitting at my mother's dining room table," he said.

The air became thick, I felt paralyzed, and suddenly it was hard to breathe.

"Are you shitting me?" I whisper in anger. Oh my God, he wins again "It's Easter Sunday for Christ sakes," I said a little louder. My head is reeling, my wedding picture is hanging on the wall in there! He knows where he is. This is my family not his! What are the shit luck chances of my mother in law even knowing him and inviting him to Easter dinner?

We go in and make a quick right, away from the dining room so no one can see us. My husband looked at me, still in disbelief like this is a cruel joke. Years ago, when we first started dating, I had to confide in him. When something like this happens to you, it's like the memories are tied to a stun gun that come crashing through your brain. Talk about an extreme mood killer in a relationship. Imagine you're wrapped up in your lover's arms, feeling so warm and safe, and CRASH here comes the memory. Suddenly, an old naked man smelling of Old Spice and showing you his hard penis. MOOD KILLER. Then you crumble into a little girl and just cry, wrapped up in your husband's arms. So many years have gone by, and it can still come back in full color as if it's happening in real time.

I said, "I can't stay," and held back my tears.

Bill agreed 100%, and we left.

As the silence cleared on the drive home, for the first time in my life, I felt strong and angry, really angry. "That bastard won again! He won't just disappear from my life!"

The incident upset me so much that I can't even remember what we ate for Easter dinner.

For the second time in 15 years, I'd step into a counselor's office. This time, if I was asked, "Do you want me to tell your parents?"

I would scream, "My parents already know! Now, I want to tell the whole world!"

It was different this time. This counselors' eyes reflected concern, caring, and warmth as she passed me paperwork necessary to process the abuse. She showed me how not to be the victim, not to be ashamed, not to sweep it under the carpet or back into the closet. She never once questioned my story. Finally, I was free, the secret was out, and I was free to talk about it anywhere! I didn't have to be sure it was appropriate timing for others. Fuck that, this happened to me. I am 100% innocent and he was 100% wrong!

At 28 years old, I had a husband, a house with a white picket fence, a business, a boat, a motorcycle, a dog, two cars, a snowmobile, and a funeral to go to.

The night before the funeral I was at a psychic party. The moving trucks were loaded up, and I was moving the salon to its new location. I was excited to hear what she would say about the success of the business in the future.

In the back of my mind was my to-do list:

- Stop at the funeral
- Say fuck you
- Get on with my life.

I sat in front of the psychic, and she took a breath and said, "I see boxes everywhere! Seems exciting and positive. Are you moving?"

I smiled and thought, yeah, this is so clear! A great decision to move the salon to a bigger location!

Then she stopped. She closed her eyes and a confused and concerned wrinkle came across her forehead. "Who is Richard?" she said. "He's just passed on and is here. He wants to say he doesn't know why some people didn't like him. He doesn't know what he did wrong."

I froze.

No one knew I was going to that funeral for Richard aka "Dick." What! What? The silent movie started in my head again. Eighteen years had passed, yet the hauntings were still clear, still no justice, and now his goddamn ghost wanted to know what the hell he did wrong?

I had no words. She moved on and rambled on about love, happiness and careers. Her voice trailed off into silence as the noises in my head got louder. I felt so confused. The swirling in my head turned into a silent tornado of alphabet soup. Why was this asshole still winning?

I imagined standing over the casket. Finally, I had the upper hand! *Who wins now, asshole? Yes, I win! ...all walls*

down…no closets! I get to stand over the casket for the last word. Society and the justice system can't let you win this time. It's over. Finally.

That was the stage I set as I entered the funeral home. I was there to celebrate, in a sense. I won't deny it. That man had taken every bit of trust I'd had in adults. But as I walked in, I felt the innocence of that little girl I'd been. Suddenly, I had long brown hair parted down the middle and was awkwardly dressed in whatever fashion the cool kids dictated.

I struggled, then faded back into today's self, casually dressed because he didn't deserve formal attire. I'd wanted to bring a bouquet of black roses for the casket, but he didn't deserve that either.

Wait. Why are all these people here? To mourn him? What?

I wanted to pull down a movie screen for all of the people milling through the room—the people who knew my family, my parents —a big screen viewing of a movie that would make them all shudder, make them see what an asshole this guy was.

This was harder than I thought. I quickly reverted back to that shy little girl. I wondered how many other victims where here?

I made my way past family friends and strangers. Quickly realizing that I wasn't comfortable with small talk or ideal funeral chatter! I imagined if one of them stopped me and asked how I knew Dick, and I inwardly chuckled at how appropriate that name was. If someone asked, what would I say?

I could hear my voice very calming and matter-of-factly saying, "Well, he molested me when I was ten years old on several occasions." Then, I'd point around the room to his daughter and my cousin and my other cousin and my other cousin and say, *"I'm 100% sure he also molested them, as well. Nice seeing you. Tell everyone I said hi."* and I'd walk out.

But instead of that scenario, I walked to the casket, stood over him and said silently, "I have the last word fucker and you will now not be able to hurt anyone again."

I walked out, climbed into my truck, took a deep breath, and pulled out of the parking lot of the funeral home as the AC/DC song "Hell's Bells" came on the radio. I found myself laughing and crying, as I turned it up so loud the windows rattled. I sang along:

Hell's Bells
Yeah, Hell's Bells
You got me ringing Hell's Bells
My temperature's high, Hell's Bells
My foot pressing on the gas, I headed for home.

*To acquire true self-power, you have to feel beneath no one,
be immune to criticism and be fearless.*

~Deepak Chopra

CHAPTER 5

If These Shoes Could Talk

MAYBE 1999 WAS the beginning of independence at age 33 and not a mid-life crisis as everyone else tagged my life, but for sure I was enthralled in one of life's turning points. One of those moments that the world has an opinion and you feel like you may be from another planet.

Enter Rudy, a fifty-two-year-old flamboyant florist who moonlighted as a pageant coach. He wore a size 22 purple sequin jacket and was always followed around by his biggest fan: his mom. Shirley doted on him like he was a toddler, always with a look of pride in her eyes.

Rudy was a family friend and had started coaching pageant queens for fun. He had seen a winner all the way from learning the initial runway walk to being crowned Mrs. New Hampshire America in 1997. Rudy loved the thrill of a girlie competition! He would say, "I don't care if you're walking down the hall of your hotel to get ice at 3 am. You must always have your lipstick and stilettos on!" If he had his way, you'd be sprinkling pink glitter all the way to the ice machine!

"Come on, Shelly," he'd say, "it will be great press for the salon. The local newspapers will be writing articles about your success. What would be better for business than a beauty queen who owns a salon!" He was always out of breath, full of excitement. "And when you take the crown, more and more publicity about you and the Water's Edge Salon will spread like wild fire."

Not knowing what I was getting into, I said, "Yes."

Ooohhh, let the games begin. I felt like Sandra Bullock being transformed in that *Miss Congeniality* movie, and boy, Rudy paid attention to every detail. I learned what to say, and what not to say. On the outside, I looked like the president's wife, all grace and stature, well-put-together; but on the inside, I felt like a little girl wearing those furry, pink plastic, light-up high heels.

Got to love Rudy. He was the epitome of pageant coaches, urging me to always have my jewelry on, my hem just perfect and extra hairspray in my Coach purse.

Everything should glitter and the hair, God the hair was always big!

Off we went to compete for Mrs. New Hampshire. If I won, next stop was the nationally-televised Mrs. America pageant in Hawaii, which would lead to the internationally-televised Mrs. World!

I realized quickly that this pageant stuff was quite a business. Entry fees of six hundred dollars plus all the incidentals. I had no idea what I had gotten myself into. You needed sponsors for everything! Three-hundred-dollar custom-made swim suits, interview suits bought used for seventy-five dollars and fitted by a tailor for another fifty, thousands of dollars for elegant evening gowns, and lots of sparkling jewelry! Rudy even convinced me that we should rent a forty-five-foot coach bus to carry all my fans and show up with massive visual impact to the Mrs. New Hampshire competition in 1998.

When I didn't win (or even place in the top five), the last thing I wanted was to get on that bus with 75 people and listen to everyone say "Aww, you are our winner," but it was my ride home.

I was thinking "I'm glad I don't have girls. I'm a grown adult and this feels so shitty."

I swore I'd never do it again.

"But, Shelly!" Rudy said. "We'll get them next year!"

This time was different. This time I trained with a personal trainer, met with a nutritionist and enlisted the help from previous queens. This time I did push-ups outside in the July heat with my personal coach, who was a badass police officer volunteering his time. I didn't order croutons on my salad when I met with the former Miss America for lunch for pageant advice on nutrition, and I made note of all the other tiny not-to-be-overlooked details.

The inspiration was contagious. Clients and friends were dieting, journaling, and creating their bucket lists along with me. One client decided it was time to go back to school for nursing, something she always wanted to do, but she had stayed at home to raise her kids. THIS was the energy that my life was about, inspiring others made my life feel perfect.

Mrs. New Hampshire was the first hurdle to cross, and at that point something was different. I really didn't care about winning. I had lost weight, I felt great, and somehow, that had sparked everyone's "get up and go." That was the prize; I'd already won.

Then came the moment on stage when the winners were being announced. We all stood in a line, backs straight, boobs out, and feet posed properly like we were plastic Barbies. I drifted off, thinking *my custom-made dress is gorgeous, if I must say so myself. It fits me like a fine leather glove.*

They announced third... *wow, I'm really proud of myself to have made it this far...*then, second... *great job, Donna.* Donna had entered last year with me. I concentrated on her face, sure she was going to take first place. A sense of peace surrounded me, almost surreal.

Then the announcement. The typical gasping-for-air, surprised look that you're SURE all pageant queens' practice. Yup, that look was on my face!

Was that my name? I won? ME as the winner! What? Wow! Okay?

Well, shit, here comes the crown and the Mrs. New Hampshire sash. Ok Rudy let's do this! I guess we are going to Hawaii!

The ticker tape parade started immediately! We took over the bar at the Radisson Hotel and celebrated success that night. Drinks for everyone as the DJ played Prince's "Party Like It's 1999." Everyone danced with me as if they had won, too.

I carried the crown for eight months, then it was time to head to Hawaii and compete for Mrs. America. As the limo transported me to Logan Airport with my fans in tow, I have to admit it was a little magical. I was kind of a big deal!

We were such a presence coming through the airport. Since it was pre-9/11, a crowd followed me to the gate to see me off. Shirley had my Mrs. New Hampshire sash redone with embroidery and rhinestones and let me borrow a sequin jacket of hers to board the plane and head to Hawaii.

I hugged my little boy and heard him whisper in my ear "go get-em mum"

I was upgraded to first class, and it was comfy sitting in a cozy leather recliner, warm lemon towels to wipe my hands, wine in a glass before we even left the ground, and a meal on a plate with real silverware. And those warm blankets... I was in airplane heaven. This must be how the fancy people lived.

A little girl, maybe 7 years old, wandered over to me on the plane, starry-eyed like she had just seen a Disney princess. She confidently said "hi," we chatted for a few, and she told me she'd be right back.

Now let me set the stage. As Rudy always said, "Never leave the house without your high heels and lipstick. Don't you ever go out in public, including sneaking out of your hotel room to the ice machine."

During my time as Mrs. NH, it was game on, everyday! Jewels, sequins, hair, makeup. Of course, I looked like a Disney princess to this sweet little girl.

She came back and looked up at me with wonder in her eyes. Her tiny fingers handed me a rhinestone necklace. "This is for you," she said, "It's mine, but I'd like you to have it, it will make you sparkle even more." My heart was all warm and fuzzy, and I had made a new seven-year old friend.

But it's pretty funny when I'd get the same reaction from

a grown woman while doing a pageant gig. I'd think, *lady, seriously, go buy yourself a new outfit. You can pay a lot of money for a dress and do this, too!* It frustrated me, because I wasn't Mother Theresa. I didn't save the world. I won a beauty competition.

When I touched down in the Honolulu International Airport, the arrival lounges seemed to sparkle as all the states entrants for the pageant started to pour in. You know who everyone is because they shine with their sashes and crowns on. The tux-wearing limo drivers were waiting for us, and the first thing I noticed was that my luggage didn't match. I had five bags, while all these other Mrs. were showing up with 10+ suitcases and all were matching sets! This was the big leagues. Mrs. Tennessee, dressed in a crisp candy-apple-red suit, was surrounded by 15 matching red suitcases. Mrs. California stood out with her sun-kissed skin, copper hair and leopard luggage. It was like fifty Barbies showed up at the airport and several Ken dolls waited to escort us like we were royalty.

I took a moment to grab some strength and kickstart my confidence. I remembered back a few months before to my five-year-old son's question: "Mom, do they know who you are? YOU -ARE -MRS.-NEW -HAMPSHIRE!"

He was in the backseat of my Camaro one hot July afternoon. We had stopped to pick my car up from the mechanic, and I forgot they only took cash. The station attendant, a young kid who had just started working there, didn't know I was friends with the owner as I tried to give him a check to pay for the repairs. My kid thought I was royalty.

The second memory came to mind. I had practiced and mastered the titled pageant wave as we led the local Memorial Day parade in Windham, New Hampshire. It felt so fancy: Me, Mrs. New Hampshire, gracefully perched on the back of a red convertible with the top down.

The last memory made me giggle...It was the famed Laconia Bike Week. I signed autographs, passed out 8x10 glossies, and well, if that doesn't that make you feel like something, I'm not sure what would. Autograph pen in hand, crown on, decked out in a black cat suit with rhinestones, I felt like Hollywood was casting my gold star to install on Hollywood boulevard. My girlfriends all came to visit and get their autographed copies, and we ALL felt like a big deal.

We realized we had a secret weapon to get into the local bar, called "Nothing Fancy," that night. All the girls stood in the long line at the most popular bar at the lake. Someone said, "Okay, girl, this is a time for the crown." We all giggled as I took my crown out of the box and placed it on my head. Literally in seconds, the big bad ass bouncer looked down the line of 75 people waiting to get into this little hole in the wall Mexican joint and yelled, hey princess girl," and waved. "You're in!"

But the most star stuck moment was when I attended the Sammy Hagar concert at the Hampton Beach Casino. I brought the secret weapon and bang! There I was, backstage with Sammy, discussing his tequila business and which Hawaiian shirt he should wear on stage.

That's as big as the small-town magic of the crown was! But the Hawaii thing was something different. Ready or not, I was there!

Let me tell you what that entails, people. A pageant is a business, not just some prestigious award. You pay to enter, and the entire process is extremely expensive. Unlike other contestants who went to Saks Fifth Avenue and loaded their cars with matching Coach luggage and new outfits for every occasion, I went to everyone's closets and borrowed thousands, literally thousands, of dollars' worth of clothes, jewelry, shoes and purses for the giant facade! The process brimmed with ego and the neon arrow pointed at me as the center of attention. I wasn't comfortable with that. I like to be the director of inspiring people from behind the hair chair. Placing that magic cape on and creating their own super hero in the comfort of the salon. But dressing up and going onstage with a neon arrow pointing to me, that was out of my comfort zone.

Those luggage sets the other girls carried were their own, not borrowed from someone else, and the diamonds that adorned on their fingers, wrists and necks were their own, as well. I'm one hundred percent convinced they didn't borrow anything! Their husbands were doctors and lawyers, and they could probably afford the bit of plastic surgery to make all these Barbies physically perfect. No lines, no wrinkles, no rolls. I began to feel like a redneck from the woods of New Hampshire, or Fiona from the Disney movie *Shrek*.

One night, I crouched down in the bathroom with the water running, so my roommate, Mrs. Montana, one of the humble, not-so-fancy ones, couldn't hear me. My voice cracked as my best friend Michelle answered the phone half awake and asked if I was ok. With a six-hour time difference, I'm sure I scared her by calling at 3am her time.

"Sorry to call so late," I whispered. "I need a pep talk. The girls are about to go meet at the beach. Do you think it's possible to get some plastic surgery in the next twenty minutes?" I broke down to a sob, and then a snort, then a giggle and back to sobbing.

She said, "Oh Shelly, you're beautiful."

"I know, but I think I want some of what they got," I answered.

Two weeks in Hawaii! Appearances with the governor of Hawaii, fancy corporate dinners and days at the beach with a film crew continually filming our every move. A humbling trip to Pearl Harbor, a fun day at a water park, and a special excursion to the big island to be wined and dined. We were showered with gifts from all 50 states, everything from t-shirts to chocolates, maple syrup and teddy bears, pins, patches and popcorn.

One evening while getting ready for dinner, my roommate was Mrs. Las Vegas. We both stood in front of the mirror, applying lashes and getting dolled up for the dinner festivities. At the two-sink vanity, she reached over and poked me in my side and matter-of-factly said," You can get rid of that you know. I did."

I was speechless. *Wow, is there no personal space, I*

thought. *You poked my side as if I was the Pillsbury Dough Boy standing right next to you and then spent the next 20 minutes discussing liposuction!*

We arrived at dinner to meet a special guest of honor, a Bay Watch young and upcoming actor named Jason Mamoa. He was dressed in a well-tailored black suit, clean cut, so incredibly tall and super sweet. If I knew then what I know now, I would have grabbed his address and taken about 100 more pics. That young handsome star has become uber successful in everything from *Game of Thrones* to the hot super-hero *Aquaman*! Jason Mamoa, you have come a long way, baby.

The finale came! After two weeks in Hawaii the film crews for tv channels around the world set up. The Nationally televised Mrs. America pageant was about to begin and the winner would travel to the Mrs. World competition in Jerusalem.

On the edges of Waikiki Beach stages had been built, hundreds of chairs set up and spot lights in place. Sunset approached and tiki torches were lit, guests filtered in and directors scurried about finalizing details.

We began the show with the spot lights off as all fifty states took their mark on stage. The music started, the spot lights flashed on and you loudly heard "Welcome to the 1999 Mrs. America Pageant". The spot light shot a beam of light onto each contestant. "Mrs. New Hampshire" echoed off the water as the spot light shined bright on me. I smiled proudly in my New Hampshire state costume, a gorgeous purple gown adorned with hundreds of lilacs and a lavender chiffon cape elegantly blowing in the Hawaiian breeze. It truly felt like I was super hero in a dress that was custom made for me by one of my dear clients, Jeanne. After all 50 states where announced we exited the stage to change for round two.

Our show hosts took the stage. Down Town Julie Brown who was the host of MTV when it aired from 1987 to 1992. Man did I wish to have her hair one day. She had the biggest hair next to Dianna Ross. Co-hosting was Chuck Woolery from the 80's game show The Dating Game.

All changed and ready we waited in line for our cue. Julie and Chuck announced the Swimsuit competition. Each of us filed out in a red one-piece swimsuit and a Hawaiian sarong to match. One by one we stopped at the microphone stating our name and where we were from. One step and pivot we dropped our sarong and modeled for the audience and then marched back into place. Again all 50 states accounted for standing on stage in a sea of red swimsuits with an orange Hawaiian sunset behind us.

Off the stage we went as the Hawaiian fire dancers took stage to entertain the guests. This gave us enough time to change for the final round and find out who was the next Mrs. America.

Final round. Our beautiful gowns sparkled in the light of the tiki torches as we got ready to take to the stage. Gowns of all colors, Christmas Red, sapphire Blue, wedding White, pretty Pink, and passionate Purple. From mermaid cut dresses, Cinderella shaped ball gowns and sexy flowing chiffon sheaths, everyone's dress was magnificent.

Different from the Mrs. New Hampshire pageants, they race right to the runner up and then straight to announcing the 1999 Mrs. America. Before you even realize it, they are crowning and announcing the winner. It leaves you stunned for a moment. We all fade away as the spot light is on the winner.

This lifestyle left me star struck and feeling fancy, I felt let down when suddenly it was over. I felt like it was the last curtain call and the lights in my soul dimmed.

Something very real inside of me changed as I boarded the plane home. I felt a little like Cinderella and I had lost my glass slipper and the colorful magic was fading away. I was on top of the world, but somehow, I felt alone. I second guessed myself. Was my ego getting in the way? I felt like a movie star, but the sad truth became clear. I wasn't happy. How could I be flying high and feel like I was crashing all at the same time? I had purchased the "starter kit of life," the man sitting next to me was my husband, and we were flying home to our house, our son, and our life.

In that instant, I realized this "starter kit" of life doesn't come with any guarantees. We became status quo, good enough. I liked the feeling of adventure and excitement. But the truth of it for me was that the experience of pageant life for the past two years had built my ego to follow through with the courage to get a divorce.

Little did I know that the shiny plastic facade Rudy taught me to erect really had done something. I realized life had so much more to offer. The pageant was a commercialized process, not genuine to me, but it taught me how to feel like a winner--on the outside. The outside did not match the inside. My proverbial rocket ship of life was taking off, and I could see my old life being left behind.

I was ok with that.

I wanted more.

What lies behind you
And
what lies in front of you
pales in comparison
to what lies inside of you.

~Ralph Waldo Emerson

CHAPTER 6

Undoing the Starter Kit

I DON'T KNOW if it starts as a child with the story books we read or the tv shows we watched, but society sets a standard and we follow it like a herd of sheep. Who is the shepherd? Who gave him the map and the list of goods? This is what I call the starter kit, the check list of life.

Graduate high school

Attend college

Find a husband

Get married

Buy a house

Get a dog

Have a kid or two

Get a bank account

Buy a car/boat/motorcycle/snowmobile/ a riding lawn

mower...

and open a business

I must have hit yes somewhere on the keyboard of life, and as fast as Amazon delivers to your door step, I was knee deep in the starter kit of life. My business was growing and I was passionate about my career. The salon was soon moving to its third location. Everything was going along as planned.

One Saturday morning, I woke up and got ready to head to the salon and I felt like a stranger in my own home. At work I was all in, but at home, I felt like a paper doll going through the motions. I had it all, but something wasn't right. I wanted to fix it, but I wasn't even sure when it got broken. I no longer felt like my best friend was beside me. The feeling was odd, because I felt stronger and stronger, but as one, not as two.

As if I was reincarnated as Joan of Arc, I started the crusade to tear down that starter kit of life, all the things life and society tell you must have to be "happy and successful."

The next few years were tough. I asked my husband to leave, and worked my ass off at the salon, sometimes wearing blue sunglasses. Everyone thought it was "Shelly" being fashionably cool, but the truth was, it masked my red swollen puffy eyes. Crying became a morning ritual, usually in the car heading to work.

Then the gossip world went into overdrive with stories about what was going on. All I could hear was judgement...

It went to her head winning that pageant, Mrs. New Hampshire!

She had it all, a perfect little world!

Has she lost her mind?

She kicked her husband out with nothing but his socks!

Stay for the kid!

I was searching frantically for the love I had lost somewhere. I wanted balance and simplicity with adventure thrown in. But life seemed to be taking me full speed down the wrong road. I felt like I was recklessly driving an old Ford pickup as fast as it would go down a dirt road. Dust billowed everywhere as the truck started to fish-tale and boxes flew out of the bed. I intentionally didn't look in the rearview mirror, but I began to feel lighter. That imaginary pickup truck sped faster and faster in order to out-race the pain following me. I filled every moment with things, stuff, empty events, because the fear of failure was on my heels. I started to build a suit of armor and imagined a virtual-badge on my chest that said, "I'm

OK," yet the truth was that if I stopped for a second, I would crumble.

I needed to be strong, at peace and full of happiness, all that would propel me to be a great mom and a successful business owner...those two things were the most important to me in my new customized life kit. *Keep your guard up, be strong and battle society's must haves,* I would tell myself.

I bought a Camaro with a Corvette engine...it was my battleship.

I bought a condo...my castle.

I got a divorce... my independence.

I bought a motorcycle...wild freedom to ride.

I went sky diving ...my fearlessness.

I volunteered to be a nude model...my recklessness.

And I buried myself in work ...my success.

The salon had moved to an even bigger location. My passion for my business and my growth cycle surged every five years. First location three-hundred square feet, second location eighteen-hundred square feet and now third location with three thousand square feet. I started a teaching job to supplement my income, and then the salon took a turn and was being swallowed up by a big move and fit-up costs. After 10 years, my empire was close to bankruptcy, the economy was crashing and the 9/11 tragedy devastated the world.

Still, I drove my T-top white Camaro with the vanity plate *Inspyr* to remind myself and everyone else that I was going to be ok. I played Christina Aguilera's angry "Fighter" song loud and then switched to classical. I couldn't bear music with words that resembled my life. But I could see the light at the end of the tunnel.

Now it was life on my terms. I built my strength and my own kit for success. I customized my life and fought for success.

When someone you love becomes a memory,
a memory becomes a treasure.
~Unknown

CHAPTER 7

My Fairy God Mother

SHIRLEY PIVOVAR, a grand dame in her 80's, never let a day go by that she wasn't dressed from head to toe in glitz and glamour. She painted her fingernails Aphrodite's Pink Nighty, used Pink Proper rouge and brushed her hair into an elegant upsweep. She was one classy hot ticket full of stories. Christmas, 2001, she handed me a gift, one which I'd cherish more than many others I'd received: a vintage triple string of iridescent Laguna crystal beads straight out of her own jewelry box. The necklace became one I've worn many times, and each time I put the string around my neck, I see Shirley's perfectly-made-up face and see her smile that would light up like the fourth of July.

We had known each other for years, both townies in the

small town of Windham NH. She started coming to the salon to get dolled up on special occasions like Christmas, Easter and Thanksgiving. I could feel us grow closer as we co-hosted a fashion show, she became my fairy god mother for the Mrs. N.H. pageant, and we hugged each time I un-caped her with a freshly hair-sprayed fancy doo.

As I read the card that was with that gift, I realized we had a magical bond that filled my soul. The words of that Christmas Card warmed my heart, it said "Merry Christmas, my hairdresser, my friend." Who knew this woman would replace the grandmother I had lost so many years ago. I didn't have a grandmother to go to lunch with anymore because she was taken by cancer when I was 13. Shirley had become my surrogate Gram.

For Shirley's 93rd birthday, I planned a surprise celebration for her. I drove to the nursing home filled with excitement to celebrate her birthday, and as I rounded the corner of the beautiful stone gate of Ward Hill Estates, I saw her smile thru the window. Decked out from head to toe in glamour, her lips glossed with rose bud pink and her dark paparazzi shades, she looked like she was Jackie O.

We arrived at the salon, greeted by the staff and clients holding purple balloons. Everyone circled around the front desk and sang Happy Birthday. The candles lit up the elegant birthday cake decorated with red and purple homemade buttercream frosting.

The makeover party began. I treated Shirl to a fancy

hairdo, sparkly-pink painted nails, and makeup that made her look 20 years younger.

I took her to lunch at one of her favorite places, C&K restaurant, a little mom-and-pop casual restaurant that she frequented. The restaurant owners, a middle-aged Greek couple, greeted Shirley like she was royalty. I announced it was her birthday celebration and asked her how she felt. She sang loudly, "Like a queen!"

We ordered our lunch. Shirl warmed up with some homemade corn chowder and I ordered lamb chops, a dish my grandmother would serve every time we were together.

I let her know I had one more surprise, and she said, "No, you've done enough."

Of course, I replied with a smirk, "Too late."

She gave me a disapproving grin and poked me in my side with her pointy crooked finger, the one she just got done shaking in the air at me.

We walked outside shivering a bit in the February New-England chill. We were arm-in-arm when I turned her down the side street to see the long black stretch limo.

"Your birthday chariot, my dear," I said.

Shirl's grip got tighter on my arm, and she started to cry.

I said, "Don't cry your beautiful face off. We just put that makeup on!"

She composed herself with a chuckle and a sniffle, and we climbed into the limo where she held my hand for the twenty-minute ride back to her assisted living apartment.

She turned to me. "I need to know how much you paid for this day!"

I replied, "Absolutely not!!

What she said next will always make me chuckle. "You listen... when we get back to my house and those bitches have their faces pressed against the windows, I want to tell them how much money my friend and hairdresser spent on me!"

My heart filled with love. Man, I loved this little old lady! Shirl was filled to the brim with class and a side of sarcasm.

I never knew my grandmother's sarcasm, but I imagined it would be like Shirl's. My memory of her is through the eyes of a child, as she died so young. Cancer took her fast, and we had no funeral. One day here and the next gone. Remembering lunch dates with Gram, she would have a martini in hand and a smile shining bright. That day came, she was so sick she needed a wheel chair and could not walk, shoulders slumped, skin grey and a defeated spirit. I miss Grams colorful spirit. I wish she could have been by my side thru all my adventures from age 13 and beyond. I remember her as if she was a legend. She held that dirty martini in her hand, strong and in control like she was a movie star. She smelled of Jean Nate' cologne and her eyes sparkled in her brushed gold cat eye glasses with rhinestones in the corners. She owned every color of sweat suits from Bradlees department store, and although her feet and toes were so crooked with arthritis she sported a rainbow collection of cheap foam flip flops. She held that cigarette like a Virginia

Slims print ad with her perfectly coiffed roller set and radiated more spirit than I'd ever seen in anyone. My strength, my spirit, my sense of adventure must be handed down from her.

I never healed. I never processed. Bradlees had an eerie feeling. There was no more special Sunday dinner with lamb chops. I couldn't smell Jean Nate'. Your grandmother is supposed to be at your wedding! I remember feeling so sad that my grandmother wasn't there for my special day.

I became friends with Shirl long after my first wedding. Shirl bridged the almost twenty-year gap in my life between when I lost my gram to MY next stage of my life. I had torn down the starter kit and Shirl was by my side thru divorce and years later finding my new love. I always wanted my grandmother at my wedding, this time she was represented by Shirl.

There is always a first for everything. Over 30 years into a profession, over 30 years of stories, yet it was the first time I would speak at a funeral. Time stands still for no one. Before

I could plan Shirley's 96th birthday, the call nobody wants to get came in on an early Friday morning.

I was at camp deep in the woods where there was no cell signal, but my cell phone screen lit up anyway. It was Michael, Shirley's grandson. I immediately thought, *oh no... he usually texts if he wants to bring Shirl by for a visit.* It rang a few more times. Washington, New Hampshire is in the sticks, no cell phone tower for miles. If I tried to answer, the call would drop. I'd only hear bits and pieces. Finally, the call went to voice mail, and no message was left.

Something told me this was bad, that something was wrong. I quickly threw on some clothes and walked next door to Mom's cottage. She had a land line phone, and I could call him back. He didn't answer, but I could tell he was on the other line by the way the phone was ringing. I left a message with my mom's house number.

He called back moments later; poor Michael could barely speak. He managed to get out, "Nana passed away." My heart sank and ached for him. He said he would call later with details and asked if I would like to say a few words at the service.

I cried all weekend. I cried mowing the rolling green lawns, I cried weeding the vegetable garden, and I cried snuggled up at the camp fire. I drove home on Sunday night and cried a little more. It didn't seem real, but it was.

It has been over 30 years since I had lost my grandmother. As I am writing this entry, I realize my computer sits on Gram's decorative antique table. When I glance across the room, there is her cedar hope chest, the one that is filled with my clothes that relate to times in my life. I realize she's been with me the whole time.

Her hope chest holds past adventures, clothes from the Mrs. America pageant, a t-shirt I designed for a gym wear clothing line, stage clothes from teaching and my wedding dress. I know she's with me. I just wish I could touch her, hug her. I wish I could smell the Jean Nate' and drink a martini with her. I imagined the three of us enjoying a cocktail together: Shirley, Gram and me.

Now I needed funeral words for Shirley.

In the early morning, I sat on my deck overlooking the beautiful ocean marsh, got out my computer and started typing "The Great Stories of Shirl." With the warm sun on my face and the beach breeze blowing my long hair, all I could see was her smile. Her smile. I realized at that moment that I had over 20 years of stories to tell and thought, well, this may take a while!

I wiped my tears and started typing. I thought about everyone that had met Shirl and whether they've been touched by her like I had. Before long, I realize I had compiled a ten-minute story. Ten minutes, a good amount of time for a eulogy. I wish I could have written a eulogy like that for Gram.

My husband Josh read it, then smiled and hugged me. With a lighthearted grin, he said, "You're never getting through this without crying, but It's beautiful."

I read it a hundred times hoping the practice would get me through without crying. *I got this*, I told myself, and I cried again.

The day of the funeral, I walked towards the podium and could feel the tears coming. *Shit, come on, Shelly you got this.* I felt super fancy, but I could feel myself crumbling, even with my hair up in a French twist the way Shirl liked it and her iridescent vintage beads around my neck.

My voice squeaked, and the tears came. I took a deep breath and paused for a minute.

"Hello, I'm Shelly. Shirley would have introduced me as her hairdresser and her friend." I choked back the tears. "I wanted to share the great stories of Shirl, but that's a lot of years and may take some time."

Everyone giggled between their own tears.

"So, I will only share a glimpse of the stories in hopes that you have been blessed with beautiful memories the way I have with Shirl. This is a collection of memories that come swarming thru my mind. I apologize that they may not be in a correct timeline order. There are so many years and so much fun, but in every memory, her smile, her smile is what stands out. The way she did a tilt of her head and out came that genuine warm smile. It would always brighten my day and warm my heart every time I would see her."

I glanced across the room to see Michael sobbing, and my heart broke even more.

"I can hear her say, ,Your hair looks so beautiful up. That's a pretty necklace. How's your son? How's your husband? You better be good to him!' It was like one run-on sentence that was meant just for me. And there, there was her smile. "

"If you knew anything about Shirl, you knew

her love for fashion and jewelry. We would always say: A girl can never have enough jewelry. It didn't need to cost a lot, but it should always make a statement, and it always made her smile. When I picked Shirley up to go to lunch, she would always be ready looking elegant from head to toe, Jaqueline Smith purse in hand and Kate Spade sunglasses on. I would tell her she looked like a movie star in her paparazzi sunglasses."

I took a deep breath.

"I would always get a vision of her in her younger days, scarf tied around her hair, necklace and earring glistening in the sunshine, movie star sunglasses on, whizzing down the highway in a 1957 Chevy Belair convertible. I wished I knew all her stories."

I looked out to the gathering of properly-dressed little old ladies holding their linen handkerchiefs, wiping their tears.

"We once hosted a fashion show together. What fun! She was in charge of fashions from her boutique she owned, I was in charge of hair and makeup and her son Rudy was in charge of flowers and production. What a glamorous evening that was! Lots of glitz and glamour."

I chuckle, knowing what story comes next.

"How about the time I was fixed up by my, at

the time, 85-year-old friend acting like a kid in a candy store, Shirley fixed me up on a blind double date."

I saw the guests smile and heard their chuckles.

"Shirley planned the entire date, down to who was picking up who. I was told to pick her up and her longtime companion, John, picked up The Date. We met at a restaurant and the four of us had a pleasant but awkward dinner. Shirl would call me every day. Did he call? Did he call? I said, no, and her filter came off. Now it was her smirk, a look of disgust, and some not-so-nice words came out."

I heard some snickers from the guests.

"About 10 years ago I remember coming to get her in the waiting room of the salon. Her grin was like a teenager who's been kissed for the first time. I said, 'What has got you so silly-happy, my friend?' She replied, 'I have a date and he is taking me to Florida!' I chuckled and thought how wonderful that this woman in her 80's could feel like a flirty teenager again after losing her husband Frankie, as well as her longtime companion John, she could still feel some silly fun love. As much as everyone's lives are filled with a little heart ache, she always seemed to see the bright side."

I looked to her daughter to see her smile.

"Then there was the time we drank vodka."

Everyone in the chapel laughed.

"I stopped by her house to do her hair before a wedding she was attending, 'Have a drink with me,' she says. 'Okay, Shirl,' I said, and she placed a water-sized glass of vodka, straight up, on the table. I remember looking up at her and saying, 'Shirl! I got to drive after this!' She replied, 'The twist of lemon takes the edge off!' We laughed, and I thought I would never forget the day a woman twice my age drank me under the table!"

"Years went on, and we switched to coffee. She made the best cuppa coffee from that vintage percolator coffee pot. Her lifetime spanned almost a century. She'd seen everything from a rotary phone with a party line to the invention of the television and computer. She was amazed by a cell phone. This little device was intriguing. I showed her its power one day at the salon. 'That little thing is a camera too?' she said. We took a picture, I typed the buttons and said, 'We just magically sent that picture from New Hampshire to Boston to Michael, your grandson.' She looked amazed.

Minutes later, my phone beeped, I picked it up and said, 'Look, Shirl, Michael received the picture and sent us a message!' She said, 'That's crazy!' I said, 'Well, let's send a picture to Judy in Florida.' She said, 'And she gets it today?' 'Yes,' I said, 'in seconds!' I could only imagine all the inventions she has seen in her lifetime."

"Shirl and I always chatted about the plans for her 100th birthday. She would always say 'Why wait till then?' so, on her 93rd birthday, my staff and I surprised her with balloons and a cake, topped with a big purple 93. I styled her hair, painted her nails and applied her makeup to go out to lunch, and topped it off with a limo ride home. It was the first time I've seen her cry, and I'm grateful they were tears of joy. We sat in the limo holding hands, reminiscing about the last time we held hands in a limo."

"Two limo rides are in our story: the one I arranged for her 93rd birthday, and years before that, to Logan Airport for me to compete in the Mrs. America pageant. My coach organized a limo, and I invited a few special people. Shirl was one, and she proudly held my hand that day. She bought me my black rhinestone earrings and matching bracelet for the evening gown competition. She had my rhinestone embedded sash embroidered with 'Mrs. New Hampshire' that I would wear for the nationally televised Mrs. America competition in Hawaii. It's something I will cherish forever."

"Christmas 2011: Shirley was in Florida visiting Judy, her daughter, for the holidays. She told me before she left that the holidays are a romantic time, and if Josh proposed to me, I needed to call her no matter what time it was. Again, those of you that know Shirl well enough, know when she tells you to do something, she means it. She made sure I had Judy's number, so on Christmas Eve, she got the call. She answered the phone and said, 'So when's the date?' I said, 'Shirl, Merry Christmas, my friend, I literally just got engaged 20 minutes ago. We don't have a date yet, but probably the fall.' 'The fall,' she said. 'That's too far away. What if I don't live that long?'

"One of the most heartwarming things happened October 13, 2012. Eight months after that call on Christmas Eve, I looked up from the beach and saw that smile. Shirl had made it to my wedding."

"Her memories long before me were so clear. The stories of her husband, Frankie, playing the saxophone with The Drifters on Saturday night.

She would grin and tell the story like it was yesterday. She would say, 'Sometimes I did not act like a lady, but I still came across classy.' Like the time she walked over a banquet table to get to the restroom. Apparently, that was the shortest route, but Frankie was waiting outside the door to be sure she didn't do that again, and he would also remind her not to buy a round of drinks for the entire bar so that he would still have a paycheck left at the end of the night."

"There were more silly stories of the characters that used to stop into the motel restaurant that she had owned for years, but my favorite is the race horse invited in for a late-night snack with the jockey from the racetrack...I said, 'Shirl you had a horse come into your restaurant?' She said, 'Sure. Why not?'

"Reminiscing was a favorite thing for her. She would talk of her trips to Florida to visit her daughter Judy, how she missed her son Rudy so much, and the love of her grandson Michael that always made her sparkle. I can only imagine the things she has seen and done in her 95 years"

"I again wish I knew all her stories. I'm sure she impacted more people than she'll ever know, and as humble as she was, I know I can see her smiling right now. She was like a grandmother,

mother, sister and friend all rolled up into one very special package, and she will be truly missed"

I walked away from the podium, sat back in my chair, and when my husband put his arm around me, I laid my tear-streaked face on his shoulder, and I cried some more. I felt a ray of warmth as the sun shone through the stained-glass windows. I placed my hand on my chest and held her vintage iridescent beads, and I could swear I heard Shirl's sweet voice whisper, 'That's a nice necklace, my hairdresser, my friend.'

A beautiful lady is an act of nature,
a beautiful old lady is a work of art.
~Unknown

PART II
ADDING IN SOME COLOR...

All the hats I wore to collect a paycheck made life more colorful, more fun, more heartfelt and fulfilling. The actual paycheck was just a bonus, my job as a hairdresser was passionate and there was an endless surge of that running thru my veins. Under all those hats I was a mom, daughter, sister and wife, I was a boss, an employee, a teacher, a performer, a confidante, and a friend. But they all wrapped around the soul of a hairdresser, artist, and entrepreneur. A respected successful business associate once told me it couldn't be done. *Shelly, you cannot split yourself from being a salon owner, to a hairdresser behind the chair, a traveling educator, an on-set photo stylist, a national stage artist and have them all succeed.*

I thought, I disagree. I can and I will. I did.

Nothing is impossible,
the word itself says "Im - Possible".
~Audrey Hepburn

CHAPTER 8

Blonde Hope...
from behind the chair, my hairdresser hat.

I MET Lexi-Skye when cancer struck her. Her hair was as
thick as a forest, swinging about in girlie pony tails. She was
an eight-year-old future actress practicing different dialects
and often sang half of what she had to say. She made me
smile with her larger-than-life attitude.

My life was being a mom to a boy; I knew boy things. I
often wonder if that's why the universe put so many girls in
my path. Maybe I needed them – or they needed me. I was
like Adopted-Aunt-Shelly to so many. Whether I met them in

the salon or out of the salon, they always found their way to my chair.

Lexi-Skye was no different, but when I was called to her house for a haircut, it started a different kind of Adopted-Aunt-Shelly relationship.

Lexi's Aunt Helen --aka, Auntie Glitter, as Lexi called her-- had been a client for years. We talked about bountiful gardens, traveling adventures and simple life pleasures. Drama and tragedy were never a part of our conversations, until her niece, Lexi-Skye, was diagnosed with a cancerous brain tumor. Helen humbly asked if I could make a house call to cut Lexi's hair. She was hosting a fun party for Lexi-Skye, disguised as an English tea party. Unfortunately, I was booked to fly out of town for a hair show. It didn't seem to bother Helen, since she knew it was a shot in the dark. She looked up at me from the chair and said, "Look at you, you jet-setting, famous hairdresser."

Funny, how the universe works sometimes. A week before the tea party, I was cut from the show. I was disappointed, but then I remembered Helen's request. I smiled and looked up, "thank you universe".

I called Helen to tell her I could attend. She acted as if the Hairdresser to the stars had accepted the invite to Lexi-Skye's tea party.

The day arrived, I packed my tools and headed out for the party. I chose a colorful turquoise bandanna and big earrings. I figured hair should not be the focal point for this emotional hair visit.

Off I went to Lexi's off-to-the-hospital-for-brain-surgery tea party. As I approached the door I could hear everyone laughing, it sounded like such joy inside! Helen answered the door with a giant smile as she proudly yelled, "This is Shelly... my hairdresser!" Everyone looked up and I was toppled with hellos, handshakes and hugs. The room seemed to be sugar coated with smiles, laughs and presents everywhere. Lexi-Skye danced over to me with a bow "a pleasure to meet you Miss Shelly" I was over whelmed with a feeling of belonging. My business trip was canceled and here I was engulfed in being part of a family. I felt like I had known everyone for years, this hairdresser thing is like magic sometimes.

Lexi-Skye danced around with her tea pot singing, "May I pour you a spot of tea?" in an English accent. Everyone saw the giant white elephant in the room except Lexi. She was a beautiful eccentric eight-year-old full of love and light but that wasn't going to stop the cancer.

We drank warm English breakfast tea out of dainty, flower-covered tea cups and snacked on sugar cookies and chocolate cake. Lexi was surrounded by family, friends AND her new hairdresser. She opened every present as if it was Christmas morning. We all choked back tears and tried to stop thinking about the risks of brain surgery and a cancerous tumor.

"Woo, Nana, look at these funky hats," she giggled." Oooo Auntie Glitter feel these soft jammies." Auntie Glitter forced a smile and then the tear dropped.

"OOOO no," Lexi shouted and popped up out of the chair grabbing a box of tissues. "We will have none of that," she said as she passed out tissues. We fell like soldiers one by one. All of us trying to paste smiles but the tears leaked down our faces. The giggles started as Lexi's beautiful soul filled us up and surrounded us with hope. I thought, *this eight-year-old is about to go under the knife with no guarantees, shit she is stronger than all of us AND our wisdom in that room!*

Wrapping paper was crumbled and sent flying as Lexi opened her gifts one by one.

The finale of the party was Lexi's haircut. She acted like the Queen of England as she sashayed to the captain's chair at the head of the dining room table. Tea cup in hand and pinkie out, she said, "I am ready for my haircut my-lady."

I took a bow and pulled out the captain's chair at the head of the table. Lexi took a seat and scooted her butt back into the chair which left her legs dangling about. I draped my cutting cape across her shoulders and snapped it shut. The sadness filled me as I brushed her hair, so thick, so shiny, hair the color of sand with natural glowing blonde highlights. The color everyone sitting in my chair wishes to have. I braided her thick flowing hair into two braids and purposely did not look around the room at any of her family. I concentrated on the love and light of Lexi. Picking up my shears I cut the ponytails off, sawing thru them as if they were wood. As they fell across my hand the weight of her hair almost brought me to my knees.

I heard her take a deep breath and with a small crack in her voice, she said in an English dialect, "Well, well, my people how beautiful am I now?'

Lexi spent lots of time at Boston Children's Hospital after her eighth birthday. Lexi's Nana would send out Facebook updates. The ups and downs with chemo and radiation but there was always hope in sight she would recover and life would go back to normal. With her swollen pale puffy body and her bald head, she was a patient who sang, told jokes and spread love and light to every soul she touched even though the doctors said she was knocking on deaths door. I knew this girl had an important job on earth here, and maybe her time in the hospital helped a nurse plummeting toward burnout or a family losing hope for a tiny loved one. As sick as Lexi was she always had the gift of making someone smile. When you're young and you're threatened with death, often the people who love you most will give anything to keep you here. They will bargain with the devil if they have to.

I didn't see Lexi-Skye often, maybe 4 times a year for the last decade or so, but Lexi is the kind of person who leaves a lasting impact on those she meets. The cancer is gone and every three months her Nana would bring Lexi to the salon. I would trim Lexi's hair praying for it to go back to normal. Thick and normal, but it never did. Every three months I watched her settle into her new self. She used to always start with her dreams of owning a red spider convertible, talked about seeing the world and being a star. Her memory loss locked those dreams somewhere far far away inside her head. I didn't hear about dreams of owning a red convertible spider anymore.

Lexi acts like a 13-year-old with ADD but in reality, she is 22 now. I think we all just prayed things would go back to normal. She is a woman now and that radiation has altered her physical and mental abilities. So, when Lexi-Skye stares into my soul with her clear blue eyes and shakes her super-fine-never-going-to-be-full-again hair and sadly asks, "Shelly do you think I'm pretty?" I died a little inside. I felt as though I had no bones in my body or breath in my lungs.

"Lexi, you are more than pretty. You are so much more than beautiful, more than most people I know." I can still see her beautiful soul. shining brightly but her spirit is dim inside the shell of a handicapped girl.

Sadly, she says "ya think so? Well, I don't feel pretty," she says quietly, now looking straight into the mirror with a sadness no girl of 22 should have to bear.

My heart breaks, my tears well up.

Thankfully, her attention span is short, and I'm saved when her favorite song comes on the radio. She leaps up from my chair and breaks out into song and dance. There's that spirit rising to the top, I see a glimpse of what used to be.

Lexi has no filter. She tells raunchy jokes, uses her outside voice inside, and interrupts every conversation.

Nana is Lexi's biggest fan and has raised her granddaughter since she was very young. She is a woman who has wings growing out her back, but don't let her fool you. Her momma bear will take you out if you mess with her babies. Nana AKA Alice on the inside is everything

Woodstock was about. A cool hippie, a daredevil that enjoyed life on the edge. A woman that as she aged fell into the role of caring for everyone else, setting herself aside. On occasion I see a glimpse of her young spirit, a giddy voice and a sparkling smile covered up by years of worry weighing on her face. She's seen a lot, still fighting her way thru no matter what the universe throws her way. My guess is Nana has bargained with the devil a few times, and this time was no different. Whatever it took to keep Lexi alive. From 8 years old, a brain tumor, surgery and a few complications Lexi was given a handful of "get outta jail free cards" she survived cancer, she cheated death but her new life is filled with short term memory problems, seizures and the label of handicapped. Lexi survived cancer, but life doesn't just go back to normal. This is her new life, her path officially changed. With a precious heart of gold, I often wondered, as I did with other client tragedies: why? Why did this happen to this beautiful girl? They say all things happen for a reason, but there are times I think that's a pretty lame statement.

Hair appointments in the salon were always a trip. I

always need to give her my undivided attention. Lexi is a whirlwind of ADD. It starts as she walks through the front door, Nana in tow, and loudly presents, in her ring side announcers voice "Lexi's Here!" If anyone in the salon hasn't ever met Lexi-Skye, they are sure not to forget this day at the salon.

Today is no different and I steer her towards my chair. Though Lexi has already jetted over standing in front of the coffee bar ripping sugar packets to add to her tea. She asks me where Shadow is, and my heart breaks and reminds me of her memory issues. I consider lying and saying he is home today. My dog died over five years ago and she doesn't remember.

I get her in the chair, caped up, and we start to catch up. As I put in foils to give her some stunning blonde highlights, it's like working with a moving target. I can almost count the hairs on her head, it's so fine. Her sensory issues are intense. I need to make sure the hair stays off her face, doesn't touch her forehead, ears or any other part of her face. Off to the shampoo bowl for a fast, not too hot, shampoo and then a quick blow dry.

We were alone in the shampoo room, Lexi seemed more comfortable than usual in the shampoo sink. There was something surreal about today. Her eyes where peacefully closed and suddenly Lexi sat up abruptly from the sink. She stood, her arms flailing and a lost look on her face.

Shit, she's having a seizure!

I grabbed her in a hug and yelled for Nana. Nana came running in with fear in her eyes.

"Shelly, we need to hold her together. She's having a seizure, and she's too strong for me."

It was as if we were battling a hurricane; unpredictable and dangerous. Lexi tried to fight us and break free, but we both held her and tried to talk to her. She was somewhere inside, but her eyes went all crazy and she pushed us away. Together, we managed to maneuver her into a chair, sat her down, and both skootched down next to her.

I put my hand on Lexi's leg, and she swatted it away, glaring at me as though I was a monster going to hurt her.

Nana is speaking loudly to Lexi and saying over and over, "Lexi, you're having a seizure. Try to be calm."

Lexi then started a rhythmic type of clapping as if her body was taken over by a poltergeist that somehow broke herself free of the seizure. I felt the air leave my body and over Lexi's head, I connected with Nana's relieved eyes, and it looked she felt the same way.

"Lexi, you just had a good one," Nana said.

But Lexi dismissed what she said and swished her hair out of her eyes, as casually as if she was flirting with a boy.

My heart still raced, my adrenaline rushed through my veins, and I fought a breakdown cry. This one shook me.

Within a moment, Lexi's ADD personality returned and she paced, coughing. I got her a glass of water and watched her eyes start to recognize me.

Nana looked at me in despair, "She doesn't even know she had one."

"Nana, what?" Lexi piped up.

"Lexi you had a seizure, a big one."

Lexi seems aggravated and said, "No, I didn't Nana. Stop talking about it."

Lexi powered up her positive energy as she skipped across the hard wood floors into the next room, complimented a client on the great outfit she was wearing, then jogged back to my hair chair, spun around facing the mirror, and said, "Wow, Shelly you are a magician! Look at me!" For a split second she saw her beauty, I hope it lasts.

The only disability in life is
a bad attitude.
~Scott Hamilton

CHAPTER 9

A Rainbow of Inspiration...

SOMEDAYS I GET to be a hairdresser to a friend...although I knew Kayla her whole life. Our bond started in the hair chair when she was three and a half and as if I blinked 12 years flew by.

Kayla blossomed into a 15-year-old yearning for a boy to call her his girlfriend. She has beautiful skin, gorgeous long blonde hair and a heart of gold. She is late out of the gate and has never had a boyfriend. She sees all the other girls at school holding hands and kissing boys.

"Kayla", I say, "there is so much more to life than boys" and then I realize how boy crazy I was at 15.

Kayla, her mom, Krista, and I are walking on Hampton beach. It seems like yesterday that Krista and I were 15 walking on this same beach, boy crazy. Wearing short shorts and flirting with boys on the beach. Where has the time gone. We are now slightly overweight woman fighting Peri-menopause and have teen aged children.

I'm not sure Kayla realizes why she is different and it makes me shudder to think about a boy that would want to check off "handicapped girl" on their sexual conquer list. Kayla is special, well that sounds bad. She is an old soul, a beautiful soul. She says to her mom and I, "Listen, you guys made your mistakes, let me make mine." Krista and I look at each other roll our teary eyes and laugh. *Wow touché, fair enough Kayla, fair enough.*

I think to myself, does Kayla even know how far she has already come? Does she know her story? Does she know she knocked on death's door a few times? I was there for it all, the timeline was scary.

Krista was my high-school friend. She mastered great sarcasm probably learned from her 6 brothers and sisters. She had a handsome four-year-old son and lived in the home her husband grew up in. My son was 5 at the time Kayla was born. Krista and I had started the life's-starter-kit: husbands, kids and houses. It seemed like yesterday when we permed our hair, wore high heeled stilettoes and were chasing boys at the roller-skating rink after school.

So, there we were, married, raising boys, working full time and maintaining homes. We struggled to hang on to our high-school best friends' relationship, and now Krista was heading face first into possibly her first big adulthood nightmare at the same time I was heading into a divorce.

I wanted you to hear it from her words, I asked Krista to bullet point Kayla's life from the beginning...

*20 *Week Ultrasound is it a Boy or Girl? So excited to find out! We were surprised, but not in a good way. There was a problem with the baby; arms were locked straight, very little movement. It is a girl.*

*Sent to Boston for state-of-the-art ultrasound and a guru doctor to go with it. Prognosis is grave, we are told. Baby could be born and live for a time, but be trapped in a "black box". Decision needs to be made very soon.

*I can feel her move, different than with my son, but still she is doing quite a bit in there.

*Back to regular gynecologist; Do not feel like terminating is an option for me. Maybe counseling with a minister, Dr. suggests. We can try amnio she says – that would confirm or rule out chromosomal abnormality.

*Amnio was done with ultrasound; Kayla moved during the procedure. Well, some movement is possible, but it is involuntary we are told. She moves again, this time Dr. admits it was a voluntary movement.

*Amnio shows normal chromosomes. Back to Boston to see a Perinatologist (gynecologist + 4 more years of college).

*Arthrogryposis. This is what I think she has, dr. says. She had done her homework before we even went to see her. Not life threatening, not progressive, physical issues only. Sign us up!!!! This is a woman I will love forever and she doesn't even know it.

*The next three months are filled with several ultrasounds and trips to Boston. Kayla surprises the heck out of some ultrasound techs as she kicks their little probe off my belly. They didn't think she could move either.

*Since drama is never far away, lungs start to look like they are not developing properly; getting close to 40 weeks. It *may not be arthrogryposis, it could be something much worse. Dr. less optimistic now. Time to schedule labor; not sure if she will breathe on her own.*

*Since this is not about me, I won't tell you how much of a freaking baby I was until she was actually born!! Ultimately a C-section was necessary. Luckily, they have special medicine for lunatic mothers having a baby they don't know will survive outside of the womb.

*First thing we noticed as they whisked her away - she was missing some toes, but crying!!!!!!!!!! Lungs seem to work pretty well! A sign of things to come . . ..

*Kayla weighs in a 4 lbs. 9 oz.; intubated for ½ day or so but then she is fine. Freaking cute as hell, nose a little crooked but I tell my husband we will get that fixed when she is older. He says no, we will not. It straightens itself out over a few days. They run many tests to confirm the diagnosis of arthrogryposis, including a full MRI. Do you sense more drama?

*Kayla, it seems, has another rare diagnosis. She has an Arterial venous malformation on her brain. It does not seem to cause her any issues so we are advised to wait until she is older to have it removed. Most people who have them don't know it until at some point it bleeds out so there should be plenty of time. Okay, we'll go with that. They know better than we do.

*10 months old, most babies are mobile. Kayla says to herself: "Hmmm. . . legs that won't straighten and weak arms that won't bend means no crawling, no walking. . .. AHA! . . . BUTT SCOOTCHING!!!!! . . . . I surprised mom when I butt

scootched all the way from the living room into the bathroom while she was in the shower. I love water. Looking up at her, shower droplets dripping down my face from the spray, I am extremely cute. I even managed to get my hand into the tub to touch the water. Finally, she looks down, sensing someone is watching her, smiles at my cuteness and a few moments later hollers out to the living room "Hey Ben, . . . how is Kayla doing?" "She is fine" comes the reply. Four-year old's; never trust them to babysit."

*Butt scootching soon turns into knee walking. Much quicker mode of transportation. Many failed attempts to pad Kayla's knees which are callous and slightly swollen all the time. Oh well.

*Should she wear a helmet? we ask the neurologist. I am not sure, he says, you should consult with a brain surgeon. Brain surgeon says she should have . . .wait for it . . .. "brain surgery". The sooner the better. Kayla is now 2. Brain surgery? Seriously? Seriously. "But, but, they said we could wait . . .." "No you should not wait. It is a time bomb." Oh, well when you say it like that.

*Kayla recovers like a trooper! Her head, however, smells like HELL until we can finally give her a bath and remove the disgusting bandages from her head. She is 100% in less than 6 weeks.

*3 ½ years old. She will not walk without leg surgeries. Thigh bones are cut in half, notched and screwed back together to "straighten" legs. She is in bilateral casts. She is different.

Cranky. Won't eat. She is afraid. Don't even think of saying the words "gloves" "shots" or "doctor". Tiny to begin with, she drops from 27 pounds to 23 pounds. We are all traumatized by this experience. Casts are on for 7 weeks. Bill starts to hold her under her arms and "walk" her around. Being upright makes her happier. She starts eating again. Her favorite – worms with trees and beetles. (Linguini, broccoli and black olives). Almost ready to exhale. Casts come off . . . Kayla is fitted for leg braces.

*One day, a week or so later, I am holding her up in standing position, braces on, so she can use her play kitchen. She seems pretty stable, so I hold on loosely. All of a sudden (okay, while I am distracted), she turns away from me and takes several steps in the other direction. Tears stream down my face . . . . She is walking!!

*Now, for that hell of a hair ball of tangled snarled mess attached to the back of her head.

*Enter Shelly. Even the Wizard of Hair will not attempt to untangle this mess. Short pixie hairdo with highlights? I think so, Shelly and Kayla decide. I am the mother, I know, but what happens at Shelly's stays at Shelly's. She and Kayla form a forever bond. To hell with those gasping mothers who take issue with "hair lights" on a three-year old. She is adorable, and happy again. As are we all. Soon Kayla is walking without braces.

*Unfortunately, Kayla's upper body is seriously affected by arthrogryposis, much more so than her legs. We have gained passive flexion to 90 degrees of her elbows; she can somewhat

lift her arms up in front of her. She has figured out her own way to accomplish some self-help skills such as eating, brushing her teeth, etc. Amazingly, she loves writing and drawing. Unable to actively bend her elbows, wrists locked in neutral, and little hands with very limited mobility and function do not deter her. In school, despite many attempts by her OT to get her to write more ergonomically feasible, she is more comfortable with her way. Eventually others catch on.

*First grade (??). We are constantly fighting her legs. Her right leg wants to retreat to its former bent position. So, it does. Another surgery. Screws are placed in knee cap. Success, for now. . .. then another surgery to remove the screws.

*Fifth grade. One leg is shorter than the other, balance is regressing. Another surgery? Yes, doctor calls one evening after consulting with another surgeon. We recommend another surgery, I am told. Kayla, waiting to hear the results of this doctor to doctor consult, knowing it could mean another surgery, waits patiently as I talk on the phone. I am sorry, honey, I say. Her reaction is not good. Crocodile tear stream down her face as she bawls out loud. She has been through so much, but now she remembers going through it and what is to come. I will make it up to you, I promise . . .. through her scratchy crying voice, she says "I want a cell phone, an iPad, and... I forget what else she came up with on the fly like that. She now has both. She would have the third thing if only I could remember what it is.

*Her inability to break her fall will turn out to be the

biggest deterrent to her independence. She cannot reach her arms out when she goes down and has no defense once she goes. Her body, sometimes her head, hits hard on the ground. (Two concussions on mom's watch; one at approximately 4 and another a year or so later). The absolute worst worry that she just doesn't understand, even now at 13, is that she gets knocked over hard and her head will hit the ground first. She wears a sparring helmet in the halls at school. She hates it, but her friends make pictures and write notes on it which helps. So, this is why when I am in the same room with Dean Kamen, I approach him with Kayla in tow and pointing to Kayla's arms, ask if his company was working on any inventions that may help her. (He was, it turns out, working on an apparatus, but for people who had lost their arms). He has his assistant send me a video, then looks down to Kayla and asks "What do you want to be when you grow up?". She does not hesitate, "a hairdresser" she says. I forget his reaction, but I know he said something to her about looking into something more "sciency". (Well, that is not the word he used because it is not a word, but you know what I mean). At any rate, I wonder what his hairdresser would think of that.

*Now at 12/13 she has straight legs and although she is still pretty short, she is just about done growing partially because of her condition and partially because of the way they had to mess with her legs to make them straight. Her endurance and strength are building and her balance *improving. We are cautiously optimistic that she will continue on this upswing.*

*She has begun what I call an "obsession" with makeup. This is where almost all of her allowance goes except she seems almost as enamored with cleansers which are a good thing, I think. One snow day this winter, she emerged from her room made up like a zombie. I am proud and disturbed at the same time. Almost every day she immerges from her room with a newly inspired look. Some days I am in awe at how beautiful she has done her makeup. Kesha and Taylor Mommsen are her favorite looks, but it is her earth tone natural look that is my favorite.

See, she is special.

During Kayla's monthly hair appointment, and as another year passes before our eyes, she mentioned, now that she's turning 16, she can work. Not wanting to bust her bubble I excuse myself for a minute and go talk to her mom. I tell her what Kayla has told me.

"Can she work?" I say sad and puzzled

"Shelly", she says frustrated "I have to try to get her a job, we need to start seeing what she can do, what skills she can master for life! She will someday need to be independent."

I say "Can she work here, she can work for her "hair bill"

She agrees and I excitedly head back into the hair room.

"Hey Kayla, what about if you worked here at the salon one day a week?" Her eyes lit up!

We get her a head set and have her practice voice inflection and tone...." *Good afternoon Waters Edge Salon and Spa this is Kayla speaking how can I help you? Just one moment I'll have Tonya take care of that for you."*

She could answer the phone but would have to pass it on to Tonya the receptionist for booking, unable to efficiently run the keyboard. She could fold small hair towels but couldn't go down the stairs to get them out of the dryer. She could sweep hair but not be able to run a dust pan and broom the way we do. Thank goodness we have an automatic dust pan. She can't make a coffee her hands are too weak to hold a full pot of coffee. She couldn't shampoo hair; her arms can't lift high enough into the sink and she doesn't have the control to bend her elbows. She knows her boundary's and she is not shy, she is brave, bold and eager. She greets people assuming the world is good and people have no judgment. Her voice is confident and welcoming.

Weeks before Kayla's sweet sixteen party, she got mom's permission to be on Instagram. With my help and guidance, she was handling the Instagram page for the salon, posting inspirational quotes, interviewing staff, and posting product knowledge videos.

She found a famous blogger and hairdresser that did cool tie-dye colored hair extensions and asked me if I had ever seen her.

I said, "DJ, yes, I know DJ,"

She almost died, "YOU KNOW DJ!!!??? Who else do you know?"

She thought I was even cooler than before and that makes me all giddy inside.

A week to go before her big party. I hadn't seen DJ in a year or so, I emailed her and asked if she could email me a birthday message dedicated to Kayla, so that I could print it out for her party.

DJ goes a thousand steps further. "Can I video message her?"

I was so touched and thanked DJ, who told me she'd get it to me before Friday night so I'll have it for the Saturday party.

The video message came in late Friday night, and I played it to see what message DJ had sent to Kayla. Earlier that week , I had emailed DJ an essay of Kayla's story so she could glimpse this amazing girl.

I sat and watched the message, and I cried. Not only did DJ speak to Kayla like she had known her for years, but she also commended her for her fearless bravery in overcoming any handicap obstacle. She finished by saying that she was making Kayla some custom color hair extensions for her birthday and sending them to her!

Then the party day arrived! Kayla has more aunts, uncles and cousins than I have ever seen and a dozen friends. Kayla's mom made enough food for 150 people, and Ben and Jerry's even set up an ice-cream bar!

A typical 16-year-old, Kayla piled all her friends into her 8-by-6ft bedroom. The rest of us ate and chit-chatted as if it was a huge family reunion. Occasionally, the kids came out to get a bite to eat. One boy came out of Kayla's room, then went back with his coat all balled up.

Yikes, I was sixteen once. *Dude be a little more inconspicuous!* I knocked and headed into her room. It was

20 degrees hotter in there, because 12 kids had stuffed themselves into that little room. No one appears guilty, but I'm sure that kid just snuck a few beers back there.

I paused, realizing, *Wow, the room smells like weed!* But there was no smoke, and I convinced myself it was just on the clothes of some of the kids who'd come to the party later. They had entered the house with slits for eyelids and headed right for Kayla's room.

I flashed to a time her mom and I were 17 and headed to Hampton Beach for a week after graduating high-school. My 1969 Rambler had a secret stash of booze and blenders in the trunk. We did it, I thought, but Kayla was too young! But, ugh, she was not. She was the same age, but her disability could make an innocent adolescence experience turn tragic. If she was impaired—AKA drunk, tipsy, or stoned—she could fall flat on her face. She has no reaction time because of the lack of muscles in her arms. As she gets taller, that's just further from the ground to fall, making her more helpless than a regular teen. And we all know how selfish and catty friends are at that age! Ooh God, all I could think was that she would be left alone in a ditch somewhere.

Let that thought go Shelly, you can't always protect her.

The kids and I chatted briefly, I returned to the adults, and the party was a success. Everyone was safe, yet I still worried as if I was her second mom.

Another year passed and Prom arrived. Kayla now has a boyfriend, he is sweet, and I trust he will treat Kayla well. I arrived at Kayla's house before the prom. Her personal hairdresser, yes, that's me. Times flies from the first time I officially did her hair when she was three, through the years of highlights, haircuts, and finally, prom day.

Kayla has her Prom team: her nana, her mom and me. Kayla has already completed her makeup, Krista is getting her dressed and deciding on the best shoes (remember: with a few missing toes, she is not 100 percent stable on her feet, so heels are out of the question.) Nana was fussing around looking for the perfect little purse for the occasion. I set up my hair studio, ready to curl, pin, and bedazzle a stunning prom updo. The dainty heart shaped necklace that her boyfriend JC gave her hung around her neck. Her ears adorned sparkling diamond earrings that her nana got her for her sixteenth birthday. I loosely braided a crown with Kayla's gorgeous blonde hi-lighted hair and delicately pinned curls into a low elegant chignon. Her dress of black tulle and a bodice of gold shined just like Kayla. It was like a scene out of Cinderella and all three of us blubbered " *oh Kayla you look so beautiful*"

Prom went off without a hitch, and she arrived home safely later that evening.

Kayla has worked one day a week at the salon. A year later she is taking appointments to teach clients how to do their makeup. Kayla can maneuver her cell phone to take before and after pictures of her makeup clients. She can use her laptop to book their next appointment in the salon and surf the web on "YouTube" to find new makeup tips. She has mastered how to do her own makeup, as well as a customer's, truly without the full use of her arms or hands, which is more incredible than you can even imagine. With no bi-cep muscle Kayla's arms don't bend unless she forces them against a stationary object. So, imagine that your arms are duck taped straight and you try to go about your daily routine . It doesn't stop her, she is inspired to form heartfelt relationships with clients at the salon. She knows what makeup does for her and wants a client to feel empowered.

I think sometimes the salon clients sit in Kayla's makeup chair out of compassion and innocent pity. They see a young handicapped girl and then something magical happens, and they are blown away. She speaks with inflection and tone. They realize there is a young woman in front of them that knows her stuff. They have judged a book by its cover, and she is so much more. She is an amazing makeup artist and exceptional conversationalist. She is knowledgeable in makeup, different applications and prescribes to each client exactly what they need to look in the mirror and feel beautiful. Kayla amazes everyone with her spirit and talent every day. What Kayla can do is endless, but there are also endless things she may never be able to experience or do. Her journey has just begun, she is no longer a child. She is a woman. A woman on a mission to change the world with a handicap that will continue to try and stop her.

She is a true inspiration to all...always up for an adventure, attending college and dreaming of opening her own art therapy studio someday. Her passions always involve making someone feel better. Kayla is always helping others to see their potential. She has trained with Sheri at the salon to be a brand advisor for Inspyr Cosmetics as she works her way through college. She preaches self-love, and beyond that, she is a true lover of all people.

I've learned people
will forget what you said,
People will forget what you did,
But people will never forget how you made them feel.
~Maya Angelou

CHAPTER 10

Black and Blue Perseverance

I'VE BEEN a salon owner for over 25 years, and the staff is like my adopted children. They are family. I'm the mom, the big sister, the technical teacher, and always the Zen master for their career. This is what I call, "My Boss Hat"

Over 25 years, staff have come and gone. Sometimes our journeys took a different path, creating a new venture, following a different avenue. I've had employees for over 20 years and employees that lasted what seemed like 20 minutes. The relationships built with sometimes-talented and sometimes-they-will-get-there employees was like having several children.

I remember when I was the youngest on my staff roster, but now I am the oldest. I am grateful to have Facebook, Instagram, Snapchat, Twitter, e-mail, and the old-fashioned telephone to keep tabs on their personal and professional journeys. I try to show them the way to success and to bring out their passion, leading them to opportunity while discovering themselves. I love when they realize that expressing their passion in an amazing environment creates an explosive energy in the hair chair. It's not just hair; it's a soul.

I'm not perfect, and I can be wrong at times. My way of running a business isn't the only way, but it's my way and it works. My heart is warmed when I see someone blossom into a wonderful human being and a talented professional. Helping them understand why getting to work on time is important, knowing how a client takes their coffee and remembering a client's granddaughters name is key to the success of a hairdresser. When I see those lessons manifest in real life, I call them my proud momma moments.

Sometimes even the financial advice that I sprinkle makes sense to them. I loved the time I took all the coffee cups from the recycling bin and calculated how much the employees had spent on coffee in a week. From Dunc's to Starbucks and McDonald's, I added the cost, and discovered they'd spent $385 in 1 week! *The money wasted on coffee could add up quick,* I told them. Why not save it for a car payment, first home, saving account, maybe even to open their very own salon someday?

As I sit and write this chapter, a text comes in from a former employee. She randomly texts as if I am her one lifeline call on things like...how do you handle employees? Can I clone myself? How do I raise my prices? How did you do this? I can always hear the frustration and sarcasm in her text. By the end of her rant, I have talked Jenny "out of the tree" and she takes a breath and realizes she loves her job, well most of it!

I have saved handwritten notes, formal letters and humorous cards as if everyone who sent them were all my kids. The mementoes are stored in what I call the Warm Fuzzy Box. These memories make me proud of the young talented salon staff like they were my own child's first tooth and their A+ report card .

I have gotten a call and been asked to do their hair for their wedding day years after they have left my employment. They have shared years later that I was someone they admired and looked up to, I'm so proud to be that inspirational force around everyone that crosses my path.

I taught the staff that The Water's Edge Salon always has a way of being home for so many with its warm comfortable environment:

- The client feels more welcomed when you know

how they like their coffee or tea and the importance of always serving their beverage in a real porcelain mug not a paper cup. The attention to detail is so important.

- Our customers are greeted by name, and we always remember how they like their hair and what is happening in their life and what products are best for them. I pride myself on the customer service.
- The customer is family and the customer is always right.

The Water's Edge salon has always been a beautiful place to build memories. I spent my life in the salon, over 80 hours a week most of the time, not only with clients but also monitoring all the "backstage" details that it takes to run a successful business.

If you have known me for years or days or even minutes, I've always had a positive vibe, but there have been days my positivity dimmed. 'The Boss Hat' said in a very sarcastic voice, referring to managing people. Sometimes felt like I was herding cats or like I said, just like parenting, it had its days of frustration.

Let's talk about different crazy insane ways that employees have quit. *"Sometimes you can't make this shit up."* Man, I wish I could quit after a long tiring crazy day!

- Quitting via text...Seriously?
- Quitting by just plain not showing up...That's the coward quit
- Quitting via written formal letter...Sweet and classy but WTF!
- Quitting via voice mail ...Wow, good for you!
- Quitting with full-blown fake tears...Nice effect for when you have been secretly handing out your new business cards to the clients!

The lack of professionalism raises my eyebrow as well as my blood pressure, because somedays that turns into my problem. I'm forced into the position of pulling a hairdresser out of a magic hat to cover the clients already booked and possibly already waiting in our waiting area. I can't decide whether I feel like a disappointed mom or an enraged middle school principal!

On the other hand, some employees keep pushing the envelope until there's no choice but to fire them. Sometimes it's just a matter of who pulls the trigger first: me or the employee. I've had employee's text in, so sick they couldn't speak, but then I find out they're working that night at their other job! Then there's the one who told me her dad had a heart attack and even phoned in updates on his health while she was out of work. (Funny, I heard that the dad was at my client's house the previous night playing cards, in perfectly good health! Don't forget it's a small world.)

One chose to take a 3-day drug-induced bender and no showed for a Thursday, Friday and Saturday wedding party. That is definitely cause for being FIRED!

Another came to me to discuss the fine print they remembered reading on the application about felony charges, after being accused of being the driver in a getaway bank robbery attempt. This is where our paths parted, and although it was humorous to learn that FBI agents look the same in person as on TV in their crisp blue suits, sunglasses and secret service looking ear pieces, I really didn't need to add to my life experience list that I have been questioned by the FBI !

How about when I saw a cocky staff member stumble into a wall with his eyelids half-closed? You bet he got sent home to put his priorities in order. Running the sharp operation of scissors for the day could lead to a giant worker's comp claim, and I get to pay for that stupidity. I think not!

Maybe a few pills and vodka weren't the best breakfast choice.

Then there was the employee who didn't understand what it meant to be on thin ice. She had to Google it!

Now I believe if you can't fake it till you make it, then be honest. Tell me, "I'm sick, Shelly. I need to go home." But if you're bored, have a hang nail, or a fight with your boyfriend, think twice about your employment if you love your job.

I often joked I'd love to give a prize to the most creative call-out line. Diarrhea, you can never argue with, and I'd like to erase that visual from my brain. Lice is a good one, as well as conjunctivitis and chicken pox. A contagious disease I can never argue with, as well as the death of a loved one.

But there are excuses that are "hard to accept" like:

- I overslept-*get an alarm or two!*

- I ran out of gas- *what are you? 16?*

- I have a flat tire- *accepted unless I have heard you on multiple occasions talk about how you can't afford new tires and your skating around on your* bald tires while you show off your new Jimmy Choo shoes.

- I have a cough-*take some cough medicine.*

- I have a headache- *yup, there is medicine for that, too.*

- I have food poisoning-*nope, it was not the burger at the club. It was the 15 beers and 10 shots you ingested!*

But the all-time (so far) best excuse is...I need to wait for the plumber. My kids flushed a block of cheese down the toilet. *Now, that's original.*

Now I'm not saying they are lies, not all of them, maybe just bad choices and creative excuses, but if I need to scramble (and that takes time – and I don't have any extra!) to reschedule all the clients in your day, for the love of god, be sure your priorities are in order.

So, I've often said if you don't want to get called into the principal's office, keep your social media clean. No posts of drunken stupor, lies or other bad manners. Have some class, invest in some morals and ethics, because one wrong move, and you may be released to succeed elsewhere.

A good teacher is like a candle,
It consumes itself to light the way for others.
~Unknown

CHAPTER 11

Platinum Joy

I'VE FELT like my entire career is magical, but every great magician has an assistant they cannot live without. Mine is Sheri, and she's the only reason why I could juggle all my career avenues for the last 20 plus years. During the first 10 years of owning my salon, I was young, full of energy and ideas, and constantly searching for like-minded professionals full of passion.

Enter Sheri...13 years younger than I, she started out as a front desk receptionist, working hard every day. She came to work as if the salon was her own but never crossed a line and respected my title. We clicked and became close friends; she was my right arm and often, my left brain. She arrived in my life at a time when I was going to need a crutch and didn't even know it. In my eyes, the universe sent her.

She trained under me and received her cosmetology degree at the same time she graduated top in her class with a Bachelor's Degree in Marketing. Then my world shifted, I expanded and moved the salon to a new location, doubled the staff to 26, fell out of love and marched toward a divorce. I was stubborn and determined everything was going to be ok even though everything was falling apart.

I picked up the travel teacher job for a few extra bucks, and I think it helped to get on a plane at times, leaving my business in Sheri's good hands and getting away from my everyday reality, the part of my world that was crumbling. Through the years, she was more than emotional support, helping me get through a divorce, near bankruptcy and took over the everyday operations of running the salon while I did what I did best...be the creative and leave the business end to her. We were a team, the Shelly-Sheri show. Some people thought we were partners, others thought we were one. We often joked that we never hesitated to answer to each other's name. We were a team, we were the Thelma and Louise in the salon world.

As the Educational Director for The Water's Edge Salon, I also traveled the country teaching in salons, at hotel conference room events, in distributor's education class rooms, and for cosmetology schools. As a traveling educator,

I've seen salons small enough for two stylists nestled between Midwest cornfields to salons that staff 40-plus in metropolitan cities. In hundreds of planes and rent-a-cars, I've hit 40 out of the fifty states and have seen all kinds of salons, schools and classrooms. Teaching stretches my creativity, fills my inspiration tank and reminds me I'm not alone in this world. From a tiny classroom in the back warehouse of a distribution center to conference rooms in hotels, you always need to be prepared for everything. From lost luggage, to shipments not arriving on time, and canceled flights, I had to roll with all the punches. As I did, I realized those delays gave me time to think, learn and recharge while spreading inspiration.

One of the most beautiful schools I have had the pleasure of teaching at several times is the Eric Fisher Academy in Wichita Kansas. I have worked with Eric on stage at hair shows through the years. He is a power house of entrepreneurship with a top-notch school that cultivates uber-talented professionals.

Volunteering my time in the cosmetology classroom of my own high school is always an inspiring moment. It feels like yesterday not thirty-five years ago every time I walk the grounds of Pinkerton Academy, a college-inspired campus with the most amazing cosmetology building. The cosmetology building project was developed in 2012 and Sheri and I had the honor of being on the advisory board to cultivate and complete this grand program.

Teaching in salons is one of my favorite venues. This allows me to see the hairdresser in their own environment. I often felt like I was hosting my own humble version of the TV Show Tabatha's Takeover. Not only was I there to teach hair techniques and product knowledge, but I'd also often lead a helping hand to arrange retail displays or manage staff. I would fold in subtle hints about ethics and best practices, hoping to steer employees to success. Without yelling, screaming and tv drama I would humbly offer some suggestions to issues I saw.

My favorite salon is in a little town in New Jersey, a village of gingerbread wooden trimmed-houses nestled by a lake that looks like Pinocchio could come around the corner at any moment. That salon is run by two amazing talented women with a passion for the salon industry. They have raised young professionals, cultivated seasoned talent, and are always sharpening their craft! Their salon is the cleanest I've ever been to; the staff is like visiting old friends and the decor is ever-changing, top notch. It's always been a true joy spending time with Mary and Jacque each year when I travel back to spread some inspiration.

I love that it takes all kinds to make this world complete. Another salon in Chicago had a great respectful staff. The staff of 15 showed up 20 minutes early to class, butts in their seats and notebooks in hand, ready to take notes. Everyone! Like it was rehearsed and they all carpooled together to the class! I had immense respect for the boss and thought she must have felt like a proud momma.

While in another salon I saw...staff strolling in late, never making eye contact and plopping down in the back row with an attitude. I'm assuming their boss made class mandatory and they wanted nothing to do with that at all. I wished for them to someday be open to new ideas, I put on a great class and killed them with kindness.

I stayed true to my beliefs and continued to spread inspiration, always open to new ideas. I learned from those salons. Sometimes it was about what not to do, but I was still learning. At one salon, I overheard the staff talking negatively about the owner. It made my blood boil, because I knew they were lucky to have such an amazing leader. I wondered if they knew what it takes to run a successful business: all the things no one ever sees. Long hours in the office after the salon is closed, the stacks of bills that multiply like rabbits, and the sleepless nights of a business owner. Sometimes a strong leader has their haters, and jealousy always rears its ugly head.

At another stunningly beautiful salon in Pennsylvania, I set up for class under the scrutiny of a staff member's five-year-old daughter. She sat on the floor eating her picnic lunch laid out on a soft blanket with perfect manners. She never spoke a word, just curiously watched my every move as I unloaded my suitcase setting up combs, brushes, curling irons, and hairspray. As everyone gathered and we were about to begin, she said to her mom, "Is she about to do magic?" We all chuckled and smiled. Everyone in that room probably thought "out of the mouths of babes," because we all knew how ironic that little innocent statement was.

We are hairdressers, and yes, we do magic.

*Live your life
and forget your age.
~Norman Vincent Peale*

CHAPTER 12

Lavender Blue Compassion

THE ADVENTURES of little old ladies and gents.

Sheri and I got a crazy idea to put a satellite location of Water's Edge Salon in a local senior living community. We called the one-room shop The Water's Edge Barber and Beauty Shop, thinking we would meld together the two worlds of a beauty salon and a barber shop. We didn't realize how times have changed.

In their generation, men never stepped foot into the beauty shop unless holding an umbrella over their wife's head to walk her to the door. We are now living in a world of equality, and I didn't realize how hard this may be. It was a different world for them but they adjusted. You could still see the men hesitate sometimes as they stepped foot into the Shoppe.

We lowered our prices and opened our hearts. The frail old seniors ranged from wheel-chair-bound with smiles to canes with grumpy faces. A few were not frail at all and sashayed into the salon on Fridays to get pretty before taking off for the weekend of adventures. Some loved life and others hated the world. They ranged from to 64 and terminally ill with cancer to 100 with all their wits, as well as every age in between.

We played Frank Sinatra and decorated the salon in black-and-white prints of Audrey Hepburn, Marilyn Monroe and James Dean. We permed hair into tight curly balls and roller set gray-white hair every Friday before their lunch hour. Sheri would trim their unkempt toenails and paint their fingernails pretty pinks. We were a Glam squad to the elders.

It was heartwarming and tragic all at the same time. Some days we dreaded going in, wondering who may not have made it to another week. This was the end of the journey for some of them, and sometimes it was a short-lived relationship, but we would always leave with a smile on our faces and our hearts filled with the time we had with them as if they were our own grandparents.

Being a hairdresser has never been about the money for me. It's been about making people feel good. So, I chuckled inside when those little ladies and their porcelain thin skin would offer up a dollar as a tip, thinking I was going to treat myself to a fancy dinner that night with my husband. They were stuck in a time warp and still believed a dollar was a generous tip.

Most of them loved hearing about my travels, always asking where I've been and where I'm going next. That would sometimes turn into stories of their own adventures and about the things they still had on their bucket list.

THE APPOINTMENTS:

Friday 8:30 a.m. every four weeks-

Quinn a young resident in his sixties wore wrangler jeans, leather riding boots and walked with a beautiful hand carved cane. He was a proud Vietnam war vet. Come to find out, after chatting with this gentleman, I discovered he was my motorcycle instructor from 20 years ago. So once a month during this appointment, we discussed bikes, safety and fun.

After his first haircut, he thanked me. He had a bumpy mole the size of my hand on the side of his head. I never said a word as I cut his hair. I worked around it as if it wasn't there. He was so appreciative that I looked right past that mole. From then on, he'd stop by the Shoppe and yell in, "You on two wheels today?" as if we had been neighbors and good friends for years. That bike was the last thing he was going to give up. He always stopped by the Shoppe to let me know if there was a charity ride coming up with his bike group, Rolling Thunder. He was a proud member of his area chapter of Rolling Thunder, organizing charity events for Veterans across New England.

. . .

Friday 8:45 AM every 4 weeks

Al never questioned me while he hesitantly gave up his 20-dollar bill with a smirk. He was a frail little man. He always remembered to tell me he remembered when the barber charged two dollars. From the depression era it was hard for him to believe a haircut was 20 dollars (If he only knew my men's haircut price was 47 regularly he would have dropped his teeth out of his head). He would be sure to get the extras and every pennies worth for his 20 dollars. I trimmed his unruly eyebrows, clippered excess hair in, on, and around his ears and took a few snips of nose hair while I was at it. I imagined Al was quite the character in his day full of his one-liner jokes, sideways comments and a smirky smile that backed it all up.

Friday 9:00 AM every week

Natalie wheeled in singing *good morning* as if she was the lead in a musical. Always put together properly with a flower print cardigan, dainty earrings and her pink lipstick on. A former kindergarten teacher, she boasted about how many copies of *All I Needed to Know I Learned in Kindergarten* she had gotten thru the years. She always wanted the sunny spot near the window to cat nap while her rollers where drying under the vintage hood dryer. Her chin resting on her chest fast asleep I would lift the dryer and say good morning. Slowly opening her eyes, she lifted her head and with a smile, sang out *good morning*. She would have her check prewritten, always hold my hand and look up from her wheel chair to thank me for "making her day."

Friday 9:30 AM every week

Eileen was a retired switchboard operator who shuffled in wearing heeled tap shoes. She had crystal white beautiful hair. She preferred a dryer in the corner, because a "proper lady wouldn't be seen with rollers in her hair." She wanted a little back-combing, not too much she'd say "just a little, not like Dolly Parton," and she always quietly asked me to check her chin for stay hairs that I should pluck out.

Friday 10:00 a.m. almost every week

Lois lived two doors down from the salon. She liked to stay in her bathrobe most of the time while she smoked secretly in her apartment. Fighting depression, she often told me she wondered why she was here. She had lost a husband, and one son, while the other son battled Parkinson's disease. But she let me know on Fridays when she heard my giggles and laughter that she mustered up the strength to come in. She would be smiling inside and out when I'd hear her say, "I heard your cheerful laugh and said Shelly would be disappointed if I didn't show up today." As sad as she was inside you would never know, it was like the beauty Shoppe was her portal to the past long before all the heart ache. Dressed in a flowered top and matching scarf tied around her neck, a cashmere blue sweater, her favorite color, and white slacks, she planted a wet nana-kiss on my check and start singing along with Frank Sinatra.

Friday 10:15 am every week

Gerry was one of the blunt, non-filtered, still-proper, frail ladies who didn't sugar coat much. One day when she didn't show up, I sent Sheri down to her room to see if she was mad at me for some reason. The clients could be sensitive at times, and she didn't like when I traveled and sent in a young stylist to replace me for the day. She was young in comparison to some, set in her ways and had traveled the world. She had lived in Japan, was an avid cribbage player and had been married for 50 plus years. I never expected that when Sheri returned, it would be with a sad and hesitant face to tell me Gerry had passed.

Friday 11:00 a.m. every three weeks

Bob liked his military crop and would always say, "My kids sent me in, looking a little scruffy." He was six-five and made my hydraulic chair look like a toy. Alzheimer's was setting in, so he told me the same story over and over about his job at Raytheon and a boss he genuinely respected. Never missed a beat. Every three weeks, same story over and over.

Friday 11:30 a.m. every three weeks

Persimmon was a well-to-do petite man who always tipped with a five-dollar bill. Always had a mani and pedi and had the longest eyelashes I have ever seen. I never got to know what he did in his life, but I imagined he traveled the world and spoke several languages. He just had that air about him.

As I teased and combed perfect coiffed doo's, clippered cuts and trimmed the ear hair, I listened. I listened to their stories, accomplishments, and sometimes, complaints. They often talked about how their kids "put them there" and how they missed having their own kitchen. They complained about the food being bland and the chef not giving enough variety. We talked about children, grand-children and great grandchildren. They educated me on bourbon and scotch, and I educated them about using their iPhone. They talked of things they had never done: skydiving, riding a motorcycle or getting a tattoo, or about how they owned a T-bird but never drove Route 66, and too many times, we talked about how they dreamed about being young again.

Oh, the endless times I wanted to put those little ladies and gents into my truck and fulfill their unfinished bucket lists.

Fill your life with adventures, not things,
Have stories to tell, not stuff to show.
~Unknown

CHAPTER 13

Rolling Green Thunder...
A day in the life of a national stage performer

I'VE TRAVELED for over 20 years for a salon haircare company called Aquage. I wake early, dressed head to toe in the company color of blue and board a plane,-- or two, grab an Uber, or a rent a car and off to my next destination. Toting two blue 50lb suitcases, one filled with blow-dryers, flatirons, curling irons, brushes, combs, capes and other magic hairdressing tools, and another filled with sneakers and sweats for set up day, as well as statement necklaces, dresses and heels for show days (Well, it used to be heels, but now let's be serious: it's combat boots bedazzled with rhinestones for my tired, getting-old feet.

My clients see me flying around the country and automatically tag mine as "the glamorous life." Although some glamorous days exist, trade shows are hard work. What they don't see is the 4 am wake up calls, the eating out of a vending machine at 11 pm because you're finally done work and meetings, and all the restaurants are closed. During the day, there's also dried up convention center boxed lunches, and breakfast consists of heating and toasting our bagels with flat irons! I'm always encouraging each team member to drink lots of water so we don't dehydrate during our long days on the dusty convention show room floor. The swollen sore tired feet, burning back aches and hairspray-covered glasses with sore red eyes under them are part of my glamorous, on-the-road life.

Occasionally there are fantastic restaurants, and sometimes you luck out and the convention center is in the middle of New York City or the Las Vegas skyline, cities that never sleep and give me a glimpse of the night life. We've been lucky on occasion to have nature at our fingertips: a convention center on the shores of the Gulf Coast, a quick ride to peek through the gates at Mount Rushmore after hours, and out early from prep day to visit the Liberty Bell.

Now I have met stars of all kinds and often wonder what makes a star. I have worked with some of the world-renowned

Joffrey ballet dancers, a very humble and talented group of girls. We worked with a team to create a beautiful coffee table book combining the art of three worlds: talented hairdressers, graceful ballet dancers and a brilliant photographer with 60 images of combined art.

That brilliant photographer was the VP, the boss-man, one of the creators of the hair care company I worked for. Luis Alvarez a passionate, opinionated, talented-beyond-words, Spanish sometimes pain-in-the-you-know-what was driven. And if you showed any nugget of talent he would invest his time to polish the diamond. He led, he pushed and he tortured us with good intent.

I have co-hosted multiple hair shows and classes with the super talented Ann Bray, hairdresser of the stars. She created Evie's gold rose wig for the movie *The Hunger Games* and trained the US team of hairdressers all the way to a gold medal. Her accolades are endless, and she is a beautiful humble woman with a great sense of humor, who to this day is still on movie sets across the world creating beautiful hair. The last time we chatted, she was working with Dolly Parton on her upcoming Christmas movie.

One hair show escapade started with messing around with Ann. She was a proper woman with style, class and grace, who often had an assistant on stage to hold a tray of hairpins and hairspray. As she backcombed an elegant shape into the hair during one of her audience demonstrations, she turned to grab a pin, but her fingers touched something unlike a pin. Instead she turned to see a burly, bearded sound crew man holding a tray of sandwiches instead of her assistant. Our VP Luis had replaced her assistant holding pins and hairspray with one of our sound guys and a tray of Italian finger sandwiches.

The next thing Ann knew there was a hovering hairspray above her model's head spraying as if it was fogging for mosquitos. Behind the curtain was our VP with a hairspray duct-taped onto a long pole hovering above the curtain and Ann's model. Oh, did we have fun!

That VP Luis was quite a character when he was in a good mood, but I learned to never let my guard down. He wanted it to be fun, but at the end of the day, it was your job, and you better be game on. No slacking, give it your all and strive for more. To him, that was the definition of success.

During one hair show with a few hundred in the audience, the VP came up on stage to whisper in my ear. That always made me nervous. Was I doing something wrong? He whispered with a chuckle, "You might want to get a little more exciting; look in the back row."

I smiled, continued my performance, not missing a beat, I knew he was giving me a hard time by his word choice, his emotion and chuckle told me not to worry. Sure enough I glanced to the back row, where he stood behind a gentleman that was fast asleep! My lesson here was sometimes shit happens but never slack on your game.

There are times I've run into celebrities and have actually found some friends among them, but some are not very accessible. One night, exhausted from the show and just wanting to put my feet up, I attempted to enter an elevator at the same time as the Bravo TV personality. Tabatha from the show *Tabatha's Takeover* and her bodyguard were one step ahead of me. Several of us were in line as her bodyguard threw his arm across the door and would not let anyone ride the elevator with her. As I stood there with a fifty-pound suitcase, balancing a box of wardrobe and a handful of paperwork, I thought, *are you serious? I just want to get to my room to put my feet up.*

The TV personality Carson Kressley from the Queer Eye makeover show hosted a show for us in Chicago years ago. Excited, for weeks previous, I'd been telling all my friends and clients I would be meeting him. It was disappointing to report back that he completely kept to himself, protected by his team of bodyguards.

Stay humble is the mantra I repeat to myself all the time. *Don't ever get so big, Shelly, that you refuse to talk to people, shun them from an elevator ride or ignore them instead of offering a friendly hello.* I am proud of my humility and think it makes the world a better place. I think it was my dad that said, "We all put our pants on the same way!"

I've found my tribe of talented people... the networking of like-minded stylists across the country is amazing. We fondly called it Team Blue, the Aquage family of blue, branded that blue color faster than Elizabeth Arden's Red Door. My relationship with that network grew tenfold when I could refer a client to their next hairdresser.

A client moving to Sioux City? My friend Amy is there. Nebraska? I'd hook you up with Tausha. Florida? Go see Lala. And California? Nogo, Trish or Ivan can take care of you. Massachusetts? Check out Donna. Ohio? Becky, Angel and David depending on which part of the state. If you're in Colorado there's Richard, Thomas is upstate New York and Lesley is in Kansas. I know Sharon in Texas, Karen in Iowa and Mary in Jersey. Visit Leslie in Las Vegas, Chris in Portland, Oregon and Shawna in Austin, Texas. I could refer them to their next hairdresser. If I needed recommendations on new salon software, staffing questions or any other business challenges, I have dozens of salon owner friends across the country to bounce business ideas off of. Such an amazing group of powerful passionate people.

So, I join my team of blue. Lights, camera, action! We create beautiful models for an eager audience of hairdressers craving something new. The music starts, and I take the stage with a smile, a rhinestone necklace and a humble heart.

*By doing what you love
you inspire and awaken
the hearts of others.*
~Unknown

CHAPTER 14

Love in Color

WHILE THE STAFF, and clients of Water's Edge, as well as my family missed me during my travel, I always called New Hampshire home. The clients were always excited when I returned and wanted to hear about the adventures, and the staff always knew I had stories to share, and my family was proud of my adventurous side.

Some days I boarded a jet, flying off to beaches for glamorous photo shoots, unique locations and stunning photo studios. From the beaches of Miami to the busy streets of Chicago, I never knew what the backdrop might be. Studios in all white, fancy lights, and amazing wardrobe for a photo shoot set in the trendy South Beach Miami neighborhoods, or the 103rd floor of the Sears Tower, 1,353 feet above Chicago. Grand beach houses on the shores of Destin Beach, Florida; flashy suites in Las Vegas; and swanky hotel lobbies in Chicago's art district. The photo shoots make me feel like I've finally made it to the top of my profession.

Still, it's surreal to see my work on the front cover of magazines and gracing the pages inside. It seems like just yesterday that I was featured in the local newspaper as a young energetic business owner, and I was so excited by that recognition. Boy, how time flies. I am so proud of the road I've taken, and I cherish those small-town newspaper articles, framed and placed next to the front covers of world-renowned magazines.

My first shoot was on the shores of Destin Beach. My boss Luis, rented a beach house for the team to stay in, and we went to dinner every night at local place called the Red Bar. I was still a little star struck that I was hired to do hair and that a paycheck would come my way for something that made me feel like I was on vacation with family. It didn't seem like work; not your traditional punch-in/punch-out job, that was for sure.

We worked together like a fine oiled machine: hairdresser, makeup artist, wardrobe stylist, and photographer. We combined our talents with show-stopping backdrops and created art. We returned to that area a few times, and in July's hot sun, I learned to apply sunscreen to our model every 20 minutes, while fixing that one piece of hair when the wind blew, and in December's cold chill, I learned how to cook bagels on the space heater on the beach while we waited for the sun to be in the perfect spot.

These shoots led to images on banners that hung 20 feet up on the ceilings of the largest convention centers in major cities, and those images were used on product packaging that sat on salons shelves across the country, these photos were entered for awards equivalent to the Grammys and the Emmys in the hair world! The most fulfilling for me was to see my work make it for the first time to the front cover of Canadian Hairdresser Magazine October 2009 and then Modern Salon Magazine and Hot hair magazine in years to come.

My first nomination for my hairdressing labor of love was for the Avant Guard category for the 2010 NAHA awards hosted in Las Vegas. It was beyond thrilling to walk down a red carpet dressed to the nines accompanied by my mom and my son. My seafoam blue gown of sequins and chiffon floated down the red carpet with grace and elegance.

Five people out of thousands of entries for the North American Hairstyling Association Awards were nominated for each of the twelve categories. I sat next to Nicolas French, someone I had looked up to for years as an Avant Guard master, and I couldn't believe I was on the same playing field as he was. His client list included British royalty, actresses, rock stars, and internationally-known supermodels. That Nicolas and I were up for the same award astounded me. He was hairdressing royalty!

Clients and staff held their phones and their breath back home, waiting for the message to come through as the winners were announced. Although I didn't win the award, neither did Nicolas, and it was truly an honor to be next to Nicolas as his equal, as well as to have my mom and my son by my side during such an honored event. My profession was my life, and it took me away from family at times, so it felt really good to share it with my two-favorite people.

I was a hairdresser and an artist. I never punched out of

the job, it was me thru and thru. I lived and breathed it every day. I remember years prior, one Mother's Day I received a bittersweet card from my son. Written all wobbly in blue crayon, it spelled out Happy Mother's Day. Adorned with colorful flowers in yellow and orange, it was one of those cards a mom will save forever. But inside the words stung: "Happy Mother's Day, Mom. I wish you didn't work so much."

It took my breath away for a minute. At that time, the money mattered. I was a single mom busting to make ends meet, and I was confident in the end that I was a great mom and this would pay off. I paid closer attention to our time together and made it count. It's not always about the amount of time you have together, but the quality of time that you spend together.

In hindsight, I look back at what it taught him. It turned him into a hardworking man with great work ethics. He is strong and responsible. His version of broke is not padding his savings account after all his bills are paid (on time, by the way). I'm proud of his soft side. He is sweet to his girlfriend, respects his grandparents, and is proud of his mom.

So, when Josh, my son, needed an internship for college in the summer of 2015, concentrating on all forms of business and creativity, I knew just the person he was going to ask. His mom, me, Madre, momma, mother, ma! I waited patiently.

He left a message on my phone. "Mom, give me a call. I need to ask you something."

I was bubbling over with pride. This was it, I thought. He was going to ask me.

I picked up the phone with a brimming smile on my face and dialed. This is what I heard..."*Mom...,* I could hardly stand the anticipation, ...*do you think*...Here it comes he is going to ask me... *Luis Alvarez would take me on as an intern?*"

What? He didn't want me? I'm deflated, I've owned a business over 25 years--umm, successful for the most part. I swallowed my pride and take a breath, "Of course he would," I said.

Luis Alvarez was the VP of Aquage. I worked for Luis for years, traveling the country doing hair shows and photo shoots, and we had formed a great friendship. Josh called him and followed up with an email. Luis agreed to take Josh on as an intern on a 3-city tour...Miami, Chicago and Las Vegas.

First Stop: Miami, June 2015

What an amazing internship this was going to be, I

thought. He may not have directly picked me, but I was his proud life mentor, whether he knew it or not. He was instantly star stuck as his itinerary arrived via email.

"Look at this, Mom, I have a king room at the Marriott on South Beach! Look at these pictures of this room." He was feeling like a rock star.

His college program paid for his flights, and his Aquage internship footed the bill for the rest, off he went.

The next day I got a last-minute call to fly to Miami and do hair for the shoot Josh was on! A mother's dream: working beside my son.

Josh called. "Mom, you got called in, That's cool! Are you staying at the same hotel?"

I chuckled as I knew the company could save a buck by booking me into Josh's room. "Silly you. Move over, kiddo. I'm your roommate!"

I immediately rearranged my schedule and hopped a plane. Josh would be turning 21 in a few days, and I got to be with him! I was already scheduled to be in Chicago and Las Vegas during leg two and three of his internship, and I was ecstatic about it. My son would be on the road with me, by my side, really seeing what I do.

I arrived in Miami late that next night to a comfy king size bed with a line of pillows running down the center. I smiled, and Josh laughed.

"Stay on your own side, Mom," he said with a grin.

"I won't tell anyone. You can still Snapchat your friends

about your king-size luxury room overlooking South Beach, Miami," I assured him.

Josh learned the rock star life had its costs. Our alarm went off every morning at 5 am. I went to our dedicated hotel room, set up the makeshift salon with our team of hairdressers, and waited for our orders. Josh went off with the production crew to lug hundreds of pounds of camera equipment, wind shields and props to the beach in one-hundred-degree weather, down the stairs, through walkways, and over the sand to the edge of the ocean. My pale-skinned, 230-pound, New Hampshire boy felt hard work that weekend. It didn't matter how hot it was, that camera equipment needed to get to the beach and set up on time. No lunch breaks, no slacking and all that equipment could not be left alone on the beach; it needed to be guarded 24/7. So Cuban sandwiches, water and sunscreen were brought to our hard-working crew on the beach. Sunburned and exhausted, Josh saw the not-so-glamourous side to this life. But work hard/play hard...the boss always treated us to a great dinner each night.

One particular night was special: Josh's 21st birthday. The entire photo shoot team celebrated at Oliver's Bistro on West Ave in Miami. A trendy South Beach spot decorated in bright orange umbrellas, glowing white paper lanterns and lush green palms. All 15 of us gathered around a long wooden harvest table and feasted on fried calamari, ceviche and artisan flatbreads. We each held a glass and toasted in celebration of Josh's birthday and a successful photo shoot. Luis walked around the table to each of us, saving Josh for last tipping his glass to Josh's beer he said *always look in the eyes* as he clanked his glass against Josh's *Happy 21st birthday my friend* and looked over at me with a wink.

Our last night in Miami was another reality check that big city fun has a price. I promised Josh we would bar hop for the last night in Miami for his 21st birthday. Tausha, a friend and hairdresser on our team, joined us for the night. We chuckled as we hit the town and made Josh look like he had a girl for each arm. South beach is a world of its own. Ocean Boulevard is lined with limos and Lamborghinis, bright lights and designer clothes. The night doesn't start until 10 pm and doesn't shut down till 5 am. On our first stop, three margaritas the size of our heads, the bill came to $96. We all laughed and thought, well, we are a long way away from home and decided we weren't going too far in our bar hopping excursion on our wallets. We hit one more spot and decided taste testing every taco on the menu was cheaper than our first stop of beach ball size margaritas!

Only home for a few days and a quick turnaround: The second stop, Chicago July 2015 Hair Academy. No working outside in the hot sun this time, but the early wake-up call was the same. This time we each had our own queen size bed in the same room in a swanky hotel in the art district of Chicago. This time the photo shoot was wrapped around a two-day advanced training for hairdressers that I would be teaching with the Aquage team. Set up was bright and early in a beautiful all-white studio down the street from Oprah's office.

Josh and I headed in early with the team for set up, putting up tables, mannequins and product for all the hairdresser attendees. While we taught the class, Josh and our production film crew went out on the town for a few hours taking pictures of iconic Chicago for the promotion film we produce for the Advanced Academies. Dinner was always at a beautiful restaurant with the entire team, for a wrap up meeting and discussion on prep for the following day. The last day of the academy was the photo shoot portion...a cherry on the cake for the attendees, who got to see what goes into producing beautiful imagery. Finally, Josh got to see my creativity in action.

Home for a week and off again...Third stop: Las Vegas, July 2015.

This stop mirrored Chicago, but Vegas throws its own sparkle into the mix, and it's a whole different backdrop. Its neon lights, 110 degrees steaming hot, constant noise of traffic, amusement rides and thousands of tourists. It was amazing spending so much time with Josh. We worked hard, had fun, I felt so connected with my kid. We found time to see a few sights, gamble a little and eat some great food. Josh lost a twenty-dollar bill in two point two seconds at the New York New York casinos and decided gambling was stupid. We walked the 4.2 miles of the strip, we stopped at Paris for a drink, went to the Ethel M chocolate factory, and stood to watch the fountains of the Bellagio. The hi-lite of the trip was when a waitress at the LINQ promenade carded me but not Josh. I laughed and said, *"Put this one down in the books. How good does it feel when you get carded for a cocktail, and your son of 21 years old doesn't?"*

The shoots continued through the years. In 2016, I was blessed with the job of assisting on a shoot and doing hair for *Modern Salon Magazine* . It was the first time in 60 years of the successful magazine that a natural gray-haired model graced their front cover, 60 years! That's big in the hair world of colored hair.

We set up in a stunning all-white studio in Miami. Once again, this fine oiled machine of talented professionals teamed up. With hair, make up and wardrobe, coupled off with that extremely talented photographer, Luis. We created a fabulous team, and the magazine was ecstatic with the finished results. In June, 2016, the magazine hit the stands, and over 100,000 copies went out to salons across the country. The front cover was stunning and the 6-page follow-up inside was absolutely gorgeous.

In 2019, I was nominated for Texture category for the Global Image Awards. A collection of my work filled four pages, plus the front cover in the magazine, HOT. Images I had created years prior were still catching the eyes of magazines editors. The beauty of social media is that news travels fast and far. The nomination spread like wildfire and messages poured in. At the Beauty Changes Lives event in Chicago on March 31 2019, I was presented with the beautiful Global Image Award for the Texture category. This collection was one that taught me so much. I had mastered and perfected backcombing, I built my first wig for this shoot, created texture from the inspiration of crinkled craft packing material, and the creativity continued flowing. Inspiration was everywhere!

Now listen, everyday isn't sunshine and roses, as Rocky says. But I know half-full vs half-empty is the best way to be. What I love is photo shoots and hair shows and the excitement that surrounds them, but sometimes it's trims, retouches and just everyday hair done in the salon behind the chair. It's excitement that keeps me on the edge of my seat, but sometimes frustration sets in. Last minute cancellations, frustration with hairpiece construction ...life can't always be perfect.

There are times I need a secret weapon to turn my mood around, everyone should have something to fill up your inspiration tank. Something that reminds you why you do what you do. Sometimes that means you need to call or text a lifeline. Or find a friend that can turn your frown upside down, a certain song that lifts your spirits, or take a trip down memory lane. That's when I go to the "Warm Fuzzies Box." A box full of gratefulness!

This is where I keep cards from clients, notes from employees, Chinese fortunes, and newspaper clippings. There are wedding invites, job shadow notes, birth announcements, and family picture Christmas cards. A cassette tape of a recorded radio ad for my Cosmetology school makes me smile, thank you notes from salons and schools where I've taught remind me why I do what I do. A card from a client that I inspired to follow her dreams of being a jewelry designer. A sketch from a talented fashion designer that wanted to outfit me for stage. A beautiful hand-written embossed card from a millionaire beauty industry mogul, an icon in the industry, Sydell Miller. It felt like a note from the president, actually better than the president. Sydell and her husband Arnie built the empire Matrix.

"I know now my son and I will be fine," is a heart wrenching note from high schooler after I told the class how hard it was to continue working (both emotionally and physically) after my divorce when my son was young. That note melted my heart. The power of a story always amazed me, my story of being a young adult struggling as a single mom made a connection and gave that young girl hope as she felt lost at age 16 raising a child.

These warm fuzzies rest here while life just keeps happening. It's a box of smiles! A treasure chest of giggles, warm fuzzies and happy tears. It's truly a box of stories. It's accomplishments and kind words from people I never realized I was helping so deeply.

All my hairdressing licenses through the years of hair remind me of my creativity! Those mug shots make me chuckle as they all are showing off the "hair" of the time...you could see I took my cue from fashion to the music industry. From the eighties to present, my hair transforms from Cindy Lauper, when I proudly wore a long shag with one shaved side accented with blonde and pink highlights. My Joan Jett-inspired hairdo was a short choppy black shag. Then the infamous Whitney Houston inspired tight triangular-shaped perm, and of course, my collection would not be complete without Cher when I grew my hair long, straight and dark. Through the years, I styled my hair to look like Amy Winehouse, Marilyn Monroe, Jennifer Aniston, and I even did the Bo Derek's braid style for a bit. These boxes filled with memories are truly a celebration of my life.

Now these boxes sit displayed in my creative workshop next to pictures of my son, grandmother, brother and special friends. The boxes are filled with the reminders of all the hats I wore, the hats that shaped me. Life isn't always easy, the divot's and dents, the ups and downs, the roadblocks and speed bumps add the richness to our lives. I still have that Mother's Day card written in crayon propped up on a shelf, it has a different meaning now as I genuinely smile and realize it was all part of the journey.

Do what you love,
Love what you do
and love who you do it for!

PART III
WHAT COMPLETED ME...

PROCESSING TIME AND FINISHING
TOUCHES

Life became more meaningful, more heartfelt. I saw full circle the meaning of life; it started to make sense. Not that it was any easier but simply started making sense. I started feeling more grateful and paid attention to the small things . I started living in the moment and soaking it up.

Any man can be a father
But it takes a special someone
to be a dad.
∼Unknown

CHAPTER 15

Daddy's Little Girl

THE MORNING MADNESS class for mothers and daughters was created to build a bond between the hairdresser and the mom by helping make school mornings go a bit smoother. I started the concept simply as a marketing tool to help my newbie stylists build their clientele, never imagining what would come out of it. Creating the Morning Madness class built amazing trust with the clients, integrity for my stylists and appreciation for my salon.

I formulated and trained staff to teach moms how to make a neat ponytail, a simple braid and a quick dance-class bun. I infused the wisdom of raising a child with its successes and difficulties into the classes. I taught them what products were needed and why. The clients amazed themselves and some pretended they were now a hairdresser to the Hollywood Stars. Their stars were their kids and their pride showed as they easily completed the looks.

We held several classes, and it became a successful marketing tool for the salon but more importantly it built relationships and beautiful memories. I love to put a twist on marketing, thinking of every angle. So, for someone who's proud to be the one who always steps outside the marketing box, I was surprised to hear my brother's best friend sarcastically say one day, "Shell, what about us dads?"

"Well, what about you dads!" I said excitedly to Danny, and just like that I was off and running with an idea: cultivating a new class for dads.

We had a few single fathers who were regulars in the salon, so I set out on a mission to organize a daddy-daughter class. I couldn't believe I hadn't thought of that angle. The two dads I had in mind were best friends of my brothers. Ironically, they both had full custody of their young daughters!

My role was big sister to this group of guys that hung out with my brother. These dudes were the lady's men of their 1989 prom. Decked out in pink ruffles and gray tuxedos, it seems like yesterday that I cut their hair for the prom. It was the era of the mullet...party in the back and all business up front for these guys. Terri, Danny and my brother Bob, were like the three amigos. Driving fast cars and full of practical jokes, they grew up fast after high school.

Danny was a big dude. A blond, pierced, Fu-Manchu-moustache-wearing biker kind of guy. This two-hundred-thirty-pound, burly, French, sheet rocker was full-time mom and dad to his beautiful little girl. Breanna had long dark wavy hair, blue puddles for eyes and held her daddy's hand like he was her life-size teddy bear. She was 5 years old at the time and sat patiently watching her daddy as he pretended to be a hairdresser. His grizzly-bear hands trembled and his eyes were laser focused, determined to get an A plus in our daddy/daughter class.

As Breanna grew, Danny became her hero, her knight, her protector. He talked about class to everyone, so proud to have mastered just one more thing that solidified his role as Mom. I was honored to be part of something that made their bond even stronger.

Grammar school, middle school and high school years seemed to go by fast, and I didn't see much of them. Time flies and Danny raised his daughter, teaching her to laugh and not take life so seriously. Danny was a gentle giant with a great sense of humor. He taught Breanna manners, poise and how to be humble no matter what life throws you.

It stunned me as years passed to experience what I saw next. Eighteen years later, I sat by his bedside in hospice and held his hand, His daughter Bree, now twenty-three years old, sat on his other side. He was in and out of consciousness, medicated for comfort.

As he would come to, sadness overwhelmed him. He asked about my son, smiled and a tear fell from his eyes. Breanna wiped her Daddy's tears with a soft tissue, as I'm sure he had done so gently for her when she was little. They had now traded roles, the same look in their eyes that I saw 18 years prior, but she was now the caretaker. I said good bye to Danny that night, hugged Breanna and whispered to her, "Write a book someday. What you two have is something so special, so many people don't ever get to feel what I can see around you."

Danny lost his battle with bone cancer January 12, 2018 at the age of 47. Funerals make you realize your age and it seems more times than not we are not ready to lose someone.

I flashed back to the boys in their twenties livin' life. Sometimes reckless but free, watching them turn into dads, work hard and raise their daughters. Time was cut way too short for Danny and Bree, life is not fair and time continues to fly by.

Be thankful for today,
because in one moment
your entire life can change.
~Unknown

CHAPTER 16

#Cancer Sucks

CANCER HAS TOUCHED US ALL.

Tears shed, hugs given and the search for comforting words.

But the reality is cancer sucks...

Every Thursday at 1 PM, Jean sat in my chair. For over ten years, as regular as day follows night, she'd show up during her lunch break from the Windham police station. She was a secretary and from the proper generation, born in the 40's. It was a time when men tipped their hat to a passing stranger, you flew in comfortable seats on airplanes where flight attendants were properly-suited and called stewardesses. She came from a generation where you spent Sunday dinner with all the members of your family gathered around a big dining room table.

Jean wore a classic blonde bouffant hairdo heavily-sprayed into place. That hairspray stiffly stabilized every hair for seven days until I saw her again. She loved her kids, grandkids, the color purple and life. She had a sarcasm from raising boys and her favorite word was queer, as in jolly, long before it had anything to do with the LGBTQ community.

Too quickly that day came when the treatments made her lose her hair. Privately, behind a closed door, she asked if I could shave off the rest of her hair. Too embarrassed to be in the main room of the salon with all the other clients, the last thing she wanted was to be on display. She looked up at me from the shampoo bowl with desperate eyes. She knew today was the day she would lose her hair. I held my composure, but to this day, I can still see the fear in her eyes. We both knew what was lurking around the corner, we took a deep breath and ignored death and styled a blonde wig to fool the world and mask reality.

Jean lost her fight on July 2, 1998, only months after her diagnosis.

I was a very young hairdresser, just starting out, and Robin was the first client I had in my chair who was dealing with cancer. She wanted me to figure out a way to keep her long, blonde, flowing wig on while she rode on the back of her husband's Harley Davidson motorcycle. This was her second round with cancer, and she wasn't going to let it ruin her fun.

I hadn't met Robin during her first round of cancer, she just spoke of it like it was a memory of a broken arm, so trivial. Now cancer struck again and she was 34 years old, and still had so many more years ahead of her. Denial was her best tool. She never looked at cancer as a death sentence; it was just an inconvenience.

As fast as the blink of an eye, she was gone. My heart sank as I realize I had met this beautiful woman that was only ten years older than me a year prior. Every 4 weeks for a year was like seeing an old friend for coffee. Then that awful diagnosis, loss of all her hair, gray skin and she started distancing...six months goes by and I leave messages, send cards and think of her every day. She secluded in her last months too ashamed for me to see her in this awful state of deterioration. It was the first funeral I attended as the "diseased person's hairdresser," and the first funeral that played music during the open casket viewing.

I could hear the whispers, *that's her hairdresser* as I said my goodbyes over her casket. For a long time, all I could see was the memory of her lying in the casket and hear that Eric Clapton song, "Tears in Heaven."

As the years went on, I replaced that memory and would think of her on a motorcycle with her long, blonde hair flowing and a beautiful smile on her face.

Robin lost her fight on May 3, 1992,

A message rang in, a house-call an hour away in Dover NH to shave yet another head. I stopped at an Osco drug store on the way to grab a card and search for a token gift, something to lighten the mood. When I spotted the pink ball cap with an embroidered patch that said #*cancer sucks,* it was perfect.

Nancy graced my chair for many years, and even spent some time working as a receptionist at the front desk of the salon. She retired and moved to Dover, NH but we stayed in touch with an occasional phone call and visit, we had a special bond. She was like a big sister I never had. Her hair was long and thick, almost overpowering her tiny build. Her petite frame fit against her husband's tall slender build as if they were two puzzle pieces perfectly joined.

Diagnosed in September 2010 with Stage 4 lung and brain cancer, the doctors told her she had six months to live. Cancer had her in its hold, but she fought hard, determined to see her son married. She did it, graciously wearing a beautiful silk scarf and a smile to her son's wedding nine months later.

The cancer grew and she made the next goal: to see her first grandchild. She was determined. Olivia was born September 8, 2012, twenty-four months after the doctors told Nancy she had six months to live. Just when I thought she had the strength to beat it, the cancer ramped up with a vengeance.

I landed in Boston on a snowy January night. My husband and I had just returned from a sunny Mexican vacation, and I powered up my phone. *Bing...*a message. I heard the deep sadness in Nancy's husband's voice asking that I give him a call. Standing on the sidewalk at Logan Airport waiting for the bus, my tears ran down my face as I immediately called him back. My voice cracked as I said, "Ed, it's Shelly."

His voice echoed mine. "Shelly, she's gone."

Her son held Olivia, his baby girl, at Nancy's memorial service. I could barely make it through the line of videos. The family was surrounded by strong love. I looked into that baby's eyes, that bald baby head, and thought *wow* all I could see was Nancy. I hugged her husband, her son and held that baby girl's tiny hand.

Nancy lost her fight on January 7, 2014.

Barbara with her positive attitude, love of life and dark shiny brown hair mustered up the strength and was ready to shave her head. She sat in my chair as if she was suited up like a soldier and ready for battle. It was harder watching the desperate eyes of her 40-year-old daughter drop a tear as she held her mother's hand, and my clippers fired up. Barbara's dark thick hair fell to the floor as I watched her daughter squeeze her hand tighter and another tear fell to the floor.

Barbara fought and survived. To this day, she walks into the salon always smiling. Her cup has always been and continues to be half full. As she sits in the chair with her full beautiful dark hair we often reminisce. "Shelly I can't tell you enough how wonderful it was to have you there for me in that challenging time" I smile and we share a hug.

They say the universe only gives us what we can handle, but I've always questioned that statement. Ironically, three years later, Barbara held her daughter's hand while she fought her battle through cancer.

Barbara is cancer free since 2010 and her daughter is cancer free since 2014.

Deb disappeared while cancer tried twice to take her. She left the salon stunning, always with a new style and color, a true hairdresser at heart and promised she would return after battle for me to do my magic.

Deb was a fun, funky, former hairdresser who sauntered into the salon one day. We colored her hair a bright auburn with a super blonde overlay and cut it into a funky stacked bob. I popped off the cape and spun her around!

"Gorgeous," she said. Deb stood at the front desk, paying for her services.

I said, "Okay, friend. When do we see you back? Four or five weeks?

She calmly and strongly said, "Well that's the thing...I've been diagnosed with breast cancer. I will lose all my hair in the next four weeks." Then, still with a smile, she continued. "I'll give you a call when I get done with this, when my hair's back and you have something to work with."

I was stunned. We hugged and she sauntered out the front door. I stood there for a moment, speechless.

Deb always popped into my mind while I was working in the salon, I hadn't seen her in years. I thought of her often, sent a few messages of encouragement but never heard back. For some reason today's memory came flooding in so clear that I welled up and wondered how she was doing, two years had passed. I was afraid she may have lost her battle. As the salon doorbell chimed, my hair stood on end literally as Deb held her hands high walking thru the front door and sang "I'M BACK" my eyes welled up "I told you I'd be back, but just as one cancer healed, I was diagnosed with a second cancer and had to do treatments all over again."

I was speechless and embraced her in a giant hug.

Deb is one of my most eccentric, life-loving clients, always positive, full of energy, spreading smiles where ever she goes. She's a success in all she touches and an inspiration to all.

Deb is cancer free since 2010.

Marion was always known for her singing voice and her hippie soul. Always dressed in flowing patterned prints of purple and silvery disheveled curls framing her face. She had an extensive hat collection from vintage to eclectic. I was confident we could hide the fact she had cancer under an array of beautiful hats. We even chatted about adding fake hair to the hats edges to look like her own curly salt and pepper hair hanging down. We decided to have some fun while we got her ready for battle.

Holding back the tears, we joked, laughed and made it fun to ignore the white elephant in the room. I took the clippers up and around the sides of her head letting the gray silvery curls drop to the floor. We stopped for a photo shoot opportunity. She sported a mohawk for a selfie before we completely shaved her head. We talked of which hats would be the best to get thru this hard time and to lighten the mood we chatted about which hat she should wear to my wedding? She said "I didn't get an invitation" I smiled and said "You just got one my friend" Marion, with her husband by her side, wore a beautiful teal hat to my wedding two weeks later.

Marion is free of cancer since 2013.

Women, we cry together, but when a man cries in my chair, it brings me to my knees.

"Shell, it's not good, I can feel it," Bob said. Bob was a high school friend who came to the salon every six weeks for a haircut. I had finally got him on a schedule instead of showing up over grown and in desperate need of a haircut because he had a wedding or a funeral to attend.

Twenty-five years ago, when I met Laura, Bob's girlfriend, I remember saying to my always-playing-the-field-friend, "She's a keeper" Laura lived life fast-- racing cars, running marathons and riding her horse. But when broken ribs from a car race took months to heal, it raised red flags. She was quickly diagnosed with a mass that was choking out the heart and a lung.

Two haircuts and twelve weeks later, she was gone. Fifty-four years old and taken too soon. Now I watch Bob my high-school friend cope, and try not to ask the universe why!

In my chair having his haircut one sunny afternoon, Bob shared a heart-wrenching story of being by her bedside during her last hours, bantering back and forth of all the ways to say, "I love you."

"Love you to the moon and back," she would say.

"Good one," he would reply, then playfully banter back. "Love you always and forever."

For hours, she lolled in and out of consciousness, before passing.

Three haircuts in and 18 weeks since she was diagnosed she lost her battle, and he felt like the rug had been pulled out from under his feet.

"How are you sleeping these days, my friend?" I asked him when he finished his story.

"Ok, but really strange. I am waking up every night at 2:47."

"Do you believe in numerology or signs from the universe?" I asked, continuing to clip around his ears.

A typical guy, he answered, "Shell, wtf is numerology?"

As we were near the front desk, I type 2:47 into the computer. Google popped up, and we stood there and stared at the screen. I gasped and he couldn't speak for a moment as I read what the Google search turned up.

Shown on the screen was ... *the meaning of 2:47, 24/7 love you, I'll love you 24/7.*

His eyes filled up, and he said, "Whoa, shit, she got the last I love you in," and a tear rolled down his face.

Laura lost her fight on September 1, 2018.

Donation cans started showing up around town at every business. Attached to the cans was the heartfelt story of a four-year-old with cancer.

I read the story about the family needing help with groceries, medical bills, and about Samantha being raised by her grandmother and her aunt. I made a call to the woman who was organizing the fundraising.

I said, "I want to donate some fun, I want there to be some happy in their lives, something more than money given for groceries and medical bills."

My staff volunteered, and we opened the salon on a Monday for Samantha's private Princess Party. We did pretty pink nails and sparkly makeup for Sam and her extended family of sisters and cousins. Nana was in a private room getting a facial and Auntie was in a private room getting a massage. I was determined the two adults trying to hold this family together would get some time to escape, just relax.

Out in the other room, the little girls, ranging from four to eight dressed up in hats and boas. We had a rainbow of shades of pretty polish to paint their fingers and toes. Makeup brushes filled with glittery pink powders for their cheeks and fun blues for their eyes! We were having fun, and everyone forgot for a moment how sad the situation was.

A family friend called the Derry News and the news crew showed up to do a warm and fuzzy article on our escapades. The following week it appeared on the front cover of the local paper. A full-page article and a picture of me holding Samantha. She was decked out with a big floppy orange hat and her petite legs dangled down while I held her in my arms.

Samantha finished treatment and visited the salon on occasion through the years. Every year we hosted a salon anniversary event, complete with swag bags, sales and celebration. Each year, Samantha would show up with her aunt and nana to pay tribute to the salon. The salon always made little Samantha smile.

Ten years passed and I was doing the career presentation for the local 8th grade. Through the years, I have put together a slide show of the fun of being a hairdresser, and I showed it once again to the group. A young, beautiful 8th grader stayed after class and came up to me. She smiled and said, "You painted my nails when I was little."

I smiled and said, "You must have grown up. What's your name?" All she had to say was "Samantha." Actually, I don't even think she fully got out Samantha, and I shouted her last name with tears in my eyes. I hugged her and yelled, "Samantha!"

Samantha that little 4-year-old girl fighting against cancer was now a tall, healthy, beautiful 14-year-old young lady! At four years old her hair was fine and feathery it hadn't had a chance to flourish yet. Now her beautifully highlighted hair was long, and there was not one sign that this beauty once fought for her life. She smiled thru her long hair with shades of blonde and brown draped over her shoulder. I thanked her so much for recalling those memories for us. Just a small gesture made a lifelong memory.

Some are now angels above me and have come to me many times. I am grateful to have been their hairdresser and their friend. I have shaved a lot of heads and watched cancer and other horrible diseases take so many, but I've also been there for the fight and the glorious win. However, when I thought I had cancer mastered, the next head I shaved brought me to my knees.

Rose colored glasses are never made in bifocals,
no one ever wants to see the fine print.
~Unknown

CHAPTER 17

Her Rose-colored Glasses

THE STANDING JOKE with my mom (aka Nancy, Bob's wife, Shelly's mother), is that she is getting a t-shirt that says, "My daughter did not do this to me!" Mom has L'Oréal-box-colored her own hair for at least the first 10 years of my career. She would say she didn't want to bother me, but then proceeded to do it and ended up looking like *oh my, who did this hot mess and ran!*

Her rose-colored-glasses way of looking at life beautifully matches her porcelain soft skin. She has never been a fan of makeup, because she always says it makes her feel like she is 'made up for the casket.' She often sports dainty, simple, green dragonfly earrings, jeans and a soft Coldwater Creek t-shirt. Mom is low maintenance. No hair products, no makeup, not even a blow-dryer or a brush. She says, "I just do this," as she tousles her hands through her hair. Happy with her Oil of Olay and her Sauvé shampoo, it's always been a struggle to reel her into my world of the beauty business. Simple and genuine, she is a classic beauty at that.

In 1990, Mom gave up her Mother's Day and helped me open the first Water's Edge Salon location. I had purchased my first home and decided to open a salon on the lower level, a beautiful spot, overlooking Beaver Brook. My parents and I spent months building, painting and decorating. Dad worked on walls and installed the brick outdoor walkway, while Mom and I polished up the used salon furniture I bought. We painted the walls dusty pink, and Mom hung lacy curtains over the picture window overlooking the brook.

I cherish an old picture of my mom on a mission to turn an old white cabinet we found in the basement into an elegant retail cabinet. She was posing with her spray paint can next to the dusty old cabinet. The cabinet was only four feet tall and two feet wide with four shelves, but when I looked at it, I thought *omg. I'll never sell that much shampoo, conditioner, and hairspray!* I couldn't even imagine having the money to stock the shelves. But, fearless, Mom painted it pink, wrapped the shelves in wallpaper, and glued lace around the front. She had no doubt in her mind I would be super successful.

Hindsight and four locations later, the retail shelves have spread to over twelve feet long and six feet high, busting with lotions and potions to keep my clients beautiful. Although Mom still enjoys her grocery-store-bought Oil of Olay, she is my biggest fan.

I can't stress strongly enough that Mom possesses the thickest proverbial rose-colored glasses, ones that never really let reality in, ones that keep her safe from the craziness of the world, which is why that day at the campfire up north made time stand still.

Mom and I sat in folding chairs out in the sunshine, soaking up the great energy that our Washington, New Hampshire camp brings us both. My parents inherited the camp property from my grandparents on my dad's side, and my parents passed the cabin on the property onto me. The "up north" property includes my quaint rustic cabin with a glass fuse box for electricity, a wood stove, an antique red hand pump that, if you prime correctly, gives you running water, not to mention a dual-seater outhouse. Mom's cottage is steps away and has gas heat, running water and an old red rotary dial phone hanging on the kitchen wall. The lawns are rolling green grass surrounded by beautiful flower gardens bursting with orange tiger lilies and fragrant budding apple trees. We had just sat down, taking a break from the yard work with an ice-cold glass of water. We both took a deep breath and sighed out a smile.

She says, "I found a lump," just as if she was about to say, the sky is beautifully blue today. "I showed your dad, and he said I definitely need to have it checked."

The air stood still for a second. I didn't know what to say. I was nervous; was she? She was queen of the rose-colored glasses and always wanted to avoid confrontation at all costs, but what about now? Was she afraid?

The long moment of silence became awkward. We shifted in our chairs, agreed we had maybe an hour left to weed, and went back to our work. We spent the rest of the day not talking about it and tending to the lawns and beautiful flower gardens. There wasn't much to say, I guess, until she went to the doctor's and we knew for sure. The voices in my head swirled around like the wind, whispering and shouting all at the same time.

We headed back home after the weekend and still nothing was resolved. It felt surreal. Our family handles tragedy two ways: number one, avoid it at all costs and don't talk about it and it will go away; or number two, humor.

The weeks that followed were surreal. We were struck with the facts. She was diagnosed with breast cancer and would need to have chemo, radiation and a partial mastectomy. I phoned her daily to pull the information out of her and track her progress. The doctors wanted to hit the cancer aggressively with chemo and radiation, so I knew it wouldn't be long before she lost her hair.

I remember thinking: *My mother has cancer.* And even though that was a fact, it still didn't seem real.

During another beautiful fall weekend, we headed back to camp. The chilly new England air made the sky a brilliant blue and the fall colors were starting to show. Mom and I started a little garden clean up, raking while Dad puttered around with a weed whacker. The fresh camp air blew through our hair, and I glanced toward Mom to see her wiping at her face with a grin. Just as the doctors had predicted, her hair had started to fall out. The wind was pulling her hair out faster than Marsha Brady's hair brush.

Dad yelled, "Hey, Shell, do you know the number to the Barnum and Bailey Circus? I figure when your mom has one boob and no hair, we can get her signed up for the circus!"

Yikes, so we were going the humor route!

Mom and I looked at each other and rolled our eyes.

That's Dad sense of humor; we were not surprised. He has always had a way of joking about things that are sensitive. I guess it's his form of rose-colored glasses.

As her hair started to fall out, I gave Mom options. I could shave her head, let her borrow my clippers so she could do it in private, or just wait. I let her know through experience of doing hair over the last 30 years, I have shaved a few heads. If you wait for it to fall out, chances are it will fall out in clumps in a matter of days. Which would be less traumatizing?

I let her decide.

She opted to let me shave it, outside on her deck, in the sun, just the two of us without many words. I wished I knew what was going on in her head at that moment. Was she okay or petrified that she might possibly die? As I shaved the last few strands from her head, I realized I hated that word: CANCER.

Dad pulled into the yard from work as we were finishing up. "How you going to get a wig to look like your mother's hair?" he asked, with a smirk.

"Don't worry, Dad, it just came in. I dragged it behind the

car for a few days, then let the dogs play with it, and it looks just like Mom's hair!"

We all laughed.

The hair was now gone, shaved off, making her look as if she's ready to enlist.

We survived that moment of trauma. We were ok, for now and I drove home.

I lost it in the car. The uncontrollable ugly cry took over. I shook and bawled, mascara running down my face as I shifted the Camaro into fifth gear and headed down the highway. It wasn't that she was sick, or that I had to shave her head. It was the realization that at my age, I'd had my mom for longer than I had left with her! Almost 50 years had gone by since she gave birth to me, and I didn't have 50 left!

The irony was she looked better without hair. I chuckled through the tears.

Other than immediate family, Mom chose not to tell anyone of her condition. She continued her daily routines, weekly stops at the post office, dump and the bank. We all giggled when she got great reviews from all the townies on how awesome her "hair "looked. She giggled to herself, her little secret, no one knew it was a wig.

She made it through the rough treatments and frequent doctor visits. She had minimal sickness from the chemo and powered through the fatigue of radiation. Her hair grew back...Now the cancer was gone, but life kept happening.

Mom's brother, Uncle Ralph, lost his battle with bladder

cancer. Mom's best friend Flo beat her cancer, but soon after, emphysema took her life. Mom didn't have many friends and now her best friend and her brother were gone. Mortality darkened her rose-colored glasses.

My dad had some heart trouble, my brother had a pacemaker installed, and still her rose-colored glasses sat poised on her nose. But they began getting a little foggy.

She loves her life, but I think she wishes everyone could just put their cell phones down and stop and enjoy life simply. She's never been sure progress is progress in the world. *Read a hard cover book*, she says, *taste the rich coffee* and *smell the fresh cut grass*. Feel the warmth of the camp fire and sleep with the window open to feel the cold night air on your face. No computers, cell phones, internet, tablets or distractions just being in the moment was what she seemed to love.

Death leaves a heart ache that no one can heal
but love leaves a memory
that no one can steal.
~Unknown

CHAPTER 18

Solid Advice

I'M A TRAINED HAIRDRESSER, but some days I feel like a bartender and a psychotherapist rolled into one! I think I have mastered the art of listening, nurturing and understanding, but using these same principles on my family is a whole new game.

Take some textbook middle child traits, a few manic tendencies and the feeling of being from two different planets and you are describing my brother Bobby and I. The punches and the jabs of sarcasm are mostly silent to all but every now and then I can see someone swallow deeply and walk away quietly, family seemed to ignore the friction. Our relationship sometimes was a struggle of trying to be me and having to answer to a barrage of disbelief and questioning. It sometimes felt like a "one up" battle.

John, my baby brother, 17 years younger than I, carries a sadness in his eyes, and wonders why Bobby and I are like oil and water. My Aunt Mary wished she could give us all a course in communication. She's always looked at ALL of us as though she was the referee. My mom practiced putting on thicker rose-colored glasses throughout her life, and my dad appeared to ignore everything and went to work.

Three years in age apart gave Bobby and I enough distance that we grew up in different circles. During our twenties, we had a few close moments and we tried to be close, but it still seemed like we were worlds apart. The distance continued to grow. I shook my head at his life choices, and he built a wall of resentment about my success.

Bobby's health declined in his forties, way too young. He ignored it, balked at it and sarcastically challenged the doctors as if it was a grade school bully fight and he stubbornly continued to play by his own rules. He smoked and had COPD, he had no concern for his diet as a diabetic and he'd inherited a bad heart.

My family is so important to me, but there were times I wondered if I was switched at birth. My little brother John was my world. I never felt I needed to be guarded or to act a certain way with him. John was born my senior year of high-school. Things were so natural and we held a tight bond, so different than Bobby and me. On occasion, it seemed as if the stars lined up for us when Bobby and I walked to the beat of the same drum. Our closeness was short lived until something shocked us both like we were wired differently.

Growing up, life went on and the years flew by. Aunt Mary buried deep in her career, Mom steadied her rose colored glasses, Dad worked and looked back over his shoulder on occasion, baby brother got a wife and started a family while brother Bobby gets a pacemaker, diabetes and continues to live his life on his terms.

I decided it was time to put some distance between Bobby and I. I was always frustrated with his life choices and felt like if I put some space between us it would help. I struggled with the hot and cold of his personality. His crass brazen ways made me retreat, it was safer.

Clients sit in my chair every day and vent about family. We often wonder how siblings raised by the same two parents growing up in the same house could be so different. Or are we? Maybe it's the difference between boys and girls? I often pondered that thought. So many siblings seem to be estranged. The thoughts tortured me... why was it so hard?

How could I be a better sister? Fear stopped me and I retreated, it was safer. We are humans and we judge. We take our opinionated guns out and recklessly fire. Other family members get caught in the cross fire and it turns into one big war that no one remembers even why it started. We are all individuals. We are all human. Which means we all are one of a kind, no one is perfect.

I worked to let go of the anger I had built up over the years, and I cherished a memory of him that made me smile. It was one of the few times we walked to the same drummer, joined at the hip, and thinking of it also broke my heart, because he made it so hard for me to love him sometimes.

Out in a bar one night after a recent break up from what I thought was my true love, my Prince Charming, my wounds were still fresh, still bleeding. It had been only days after the break up, so I felt my knees buckle and the blood drain out of my face as I watched my prince walk into the bar with his new girlfriend.

Bobby stood next to me and followed my eyes, then immediately stood in front of my laser focus and blocked the view. I was paralyzed. He looked at me and sternly said, "Go through the dining room and directly out the back door. I'll meet you there."

I stood for a second, but he sternly said "GO."

My world was crushing. I felt like I had lead in my shoes, my lip quivered and my eyes filled, but I did as he said.

I pushed open the back door, and it was dark except for my brother's tow truck, which was lit up like a Christmas tree. The truck rumbled and the passenger's door flung open. "Get in," he ordered.

Like a zombie, I climbed up in the truck. He had hooked up my car and he was getting me out of there before the ugly cry came. I would have been embarrassed to the core if I'd fallen apart in that bar, and he knew it. I don't even remember talking that night, but I felt such a sense of comfort, peace and protection.

That night he was my hero, and I cherished that memory. He didn't judge me or criticize me. He just rescued me and loved me. So, I held that memory tight and loved him from a distance.

Three years had passed, and we had not talked. We had been at the same family functions, but we didn't make eye contact, and I had bowed out of a few to give him space.

Then out of the blue one day, he texted to let me know Danny, his best friend, was dying of cancer. As if we had never fought, he asked me to go see Danny. I was like the surrogate sister to four guys—my brother, Danny, and two more friends--for a short time in our 20's when we marched to the same drum.

My brother was more broken than I have ever seen him, vulnerable and sad. Although 47 is too young to die, it's often the age we get a reality check. Health issues crop up, the aging process goes faster, yet we all still feel like we are 20.

Danny passed, and Bobby now had another hole torn in his soul. At Dan's services, we stood with friends and ignored the fact that we hadn't talked in three years. It was like our difference's just disappeared.

I traveled my way through the receiving line past the picture boards to Danny's parents. It had been years since I'd seen them. Danny's mom was hooked to oxygen and battling COPD. Danny's dad had his share of health issues, as well. I passed by Danny's daughter, Bree, hugged her and said, "write that book friend". This heart wrenching journey she has been on with her Dad would surely be a best seller.

I continued to walk through the receiving line, and Danny's mom grabbed my arm. In her French-Canadian brogue, in between tears, she said, "Shellee, Bub tells me you are talking. Don't stop. Please, don't stop. Time is short."

My own tears welled up, and I promised her I wouldn't stop.

Spring came and the motorcycles came out.

Sunday was a beautiful day for a family cook-out. Bobby and I talked like we had never been estranged. It felt comfortable. As I left that gathering, I reflected on how nice it was. No fake facades, just family enjoying each other.

I glanced at my phone and pulled up my calendar. Bobby mentioned how work was slow lately, and he wasn't working much. I thought, *wow, if my day is empty, I should call Bobby and ask him if he wanted to go for a ride.* I chuckled. My calendar is NEVER empty. That's like leap year in my world.

We had motorcycles in common, and he was super proud of purchasing his new bike. I suddenly got an uneasy feeling. I didn't want to wreck what we had by pushing too hard for more, so I decided to let it go slow. I wouldn't call. I'd just let it go.

At 7 AM, a text came into my phone. "What are you up to today?" It was Bobby.

I lay in bed and looked up at the ceiling, saying out loud, "Ok, Universe, I hear you loud and clear."

I texted back: "Nothing on the calendar. Want to come over?"

"Sure, where you at?"

Ugh, I felt my heart sink. It had been that long that he didn't know where I lived.

I texted back the address and started the coffee.

I heard his bike roar in around 8, and I have to admit I was nervous. I wanted this to go great. I gave him a tour of my house, and we stepped out to the deck overlooking the lake.

"Wow," he said. "This is great."

In his heavy Timberlane work boots, faded Levi's and Harley T-shirt with the collar ripped off, he plopped down onto the new deck furniture.

Bobby was always a big guy, 5' 11", pushing two hundred and fifty pounds. He had a ton of hair but always went for the shaved bad-ass look, a moustache, a goatee and four steel hoops in each ear.

Time stood still that day. Slowly, he became more comfortable on the couch and even almost dozed off. We just talked, never ate or even had a moment to spare. The sun came up and over the house. We went from early morning to noon, and before long it was four o'clock in the afternoon.

"Wow, "he said. "This is nice." His voice was so calm and at ease, that all my guards fell down.

January 30, 2019. One year and 19 days after her son passed away, Danny's mom, Nicky, passed away. I had been making house calls every 6 weeks for the last year, a haircut in her kitchen to make her look and feel beautiful . We spent the time talking about the old days. She missed her son so much. We talked of Bobby and Danny's days as teens and all their escapades. She was sad that Bobby hadn't come to see her since Danny was gone, but I know it was just too painful, too hard for him to bear. She would always say, "How's Bub? Tell him I got a pork pie here for him." Reminiscing kept my brother's best friend, her son, "alive."

Nicky would say, "Those boys were afraid of me. The shit they pulled!"

In the lobby of Peabody's funeral home, Bobby's skin was pale and he looked weak. With a bad heart, COPD and diabetes, his health was always in question.

I gave him a hug and said, "Hey, you don't look so good."

"Yeah, I'm headed up to Catholic Medical Center to check myself in tonight, I think I need a tune up"

I hugged him again and said, "Love ya. Keep me posted."

That was the last day I talked to my brother.

That next morning, he suffered a massive stroke in the hospital and remained unconscious.

The doctors pumped him full of meds, ran tests and tried to reverse the damage of the stroke. All he had to do was respond, squeeze our hand or open his eyes.

I got to the hospital Sunday afternoon and continued to go to the hospital each day. It was surreal. He had gambled with death so many other times, but each time he came out of it like a black cat, but this didn't look good. He was running out of lives. I could feel the end coming.

Each night when I came, I found the waiting room filled with his friends. I mean filled, with up to fifty people rallying for him to wake up. I sat by his bed and held his hand, remembering that day on the deck last summer. I listened to his friends tell stories, and we all talked as if he would join into the conversation at any moment. I'd tickle his feet and he'd pull away. With tears in my eyes, I'd say, "Just open your eyes, Bobby, that's what they want you to do...just open your eyes."

Other days I stood by his bed and softly ran my fingers across his forehead. Silently, I told him to go where he would be happiest. I wanted him to be at peace. I always felt he had a small hole in his soul, and that he was always searching for something, someone, to make him happy.

I wonder if he ever knew how many loved him, even when he made it hard for some to love him.

Six long days in the hospital...

Just open your eyes Bobby. Just squeeze my hand.

The day after Valentine's Day, we gathered around his bed: my parents, Aunt Mary, two of Bobby's daughters, my brother John and his wife Erin, and my husband and I. The doctors had shut Bobby's pacemaker off and removed the ventilator. He wasn't on life support, but the nurse informed us that his vitals showed he was going to pass on his own. It should take a few hours, she said.

"What should we expect?" I asked the nurse.

She told us he would continue to look like he was sleeping, and he would breathe normally, then usually there was one last big breath. The nurses had done a wonderful job of taking care of him. He did look peaceful but the reality of what we were witnessing was heartbreaking.

I watched my mom stand by his side and rub his forehead. My dad stood by the foot of his bed, my Aunt Mary next to him. My brother John sat with his wife Erin on one side and Bobbys daughters on the other side. My husband stood behind me and engulfed me in a hug. Bobby breathed nine breaths, and the last breath sounded almost like a sigh.

I looked at the nurse and she nodded. We thought he was gone, but after 45 seconds, he breathed again. He did that for three hours! I didn't want to leave the room, but it was so tough.

I couldn't believe what I was seeing. Watching someone

die is the most helpless feeling. I felt empty and sad. I whimpered, and my husband held me tight.

Bobby took his last breath at 9 PM that night. I imagined him, fitted for his angel wings customized with a Harley logo, headed through the pearly gates. I imagined Danny was right there and that they smiled at each other and embraced in a big bear hug. I could see them turn and walk away, and off in the distance I could see Nicky. She smiled and yelled, "Don't stop talking to him!"

Life is short, time is too precious and the stakes are too high
to dwell on what might have been,
we have to work hard
on what still can be.
~Unknown

CHAPTER 19

Life is Short

THERE'S a sentimental saying that goes, "It's not the amount of breaths you take but the moments that take your breath away." Well, when you watch someone take their last breath, it changes your life.

Where does the time go? When I was a kid, time seemed to stand still, seemingly endless. You start to realize how many people are involved in shaping your life as you get older. Now I reflect back that many have made their mark on my blueprint of life. My parents, family members, friends and sometimes strangers.

Minutes after Bobby died, I started to feel how short life really is. As an adult, time stood still and I faced reality. It was ugly and almost unbelievable and I saw the clock ticking before my eyes. Time was standing still but at the same time the hands of the clock spun around the face of the clock like it was out of control.

One particular person helped shape my life as a child: Aunt Mary, my dad's sister. Aunt Mary instilled wisdom, adventure and fun in me, three elements that people would use to describe me. A hardworking career woman, Mary divorced when I was 13 and chose refuge in her heartache by burying herself in her education, gardening and traveling the world. She was (and is) the glue to the family. A strong, vibrant, fun-loving woman with a roar of a laugh.

"Get quiet," she would say to me, "what's important?"

My Aunt Mary always infused me with nuggets of wisdom. One thing she would say to me as a teenager was, "What do you want on your tomb stone? What do you want to be known for?"

At 15, 16 or 17, I really didn't know yet. I wanted to be kind to people, helpful, I wanted to be known for integrity and honesty. It always seemed like such an important question, like I was supposed to answer with..."I'd like to be a brain surgeon at Mass General."

Aunt Mary always had a way of teaching me how to figure it out myself. She instilled my sense of adventure and challenged me to think outside the box. "College or no college," she would say, reminding me it was my choice, not just the next thing you did after high school.

As I get even older, I understand more of what she really meant. Stuff gets less important. Rules are sometimes meant to be broken. Living is more than just breathing.

When we baked cookies, she would say, "How big should we make them?"

I blankly looked at her and she would wave her hands in a big motion and say, "This big "with her face all animated or she'd pinch her fingers and squint her eyes together and say, "This tiny?" Then she would toss some flour at me to break the intense thought I had on my face.

If you know the rules, you can break them. Everything was about learning, and she made it fun.

Aunt Mary lived across the street from the home I grew up in. Both my parents' home and Aunt Mary's were built on my grandparent's land. When we were kids, Dad would teach us the secret "eye spy" way to get to Aunt Mary's: down the hill, through the culvert, under the street and across the brook to Aunt Mary's. I was a kid, so I didn't think about spiders being in the tunnel under the street. It was the coolest path to Aunt Mary's.

As I grew up, Aunt Mary's adventures didn't only involve baking. We searched NH for the biggest ice cream sundae, drank virgin strawberry daiquiris at fancy bars, and had contests on who could make the longest apple peel while peeling apples for turnovers.

I lived with her for a short time after my divorce. We chuckled one day when our relationship shifted from adult and child to more like two sisters. We found ourselves both single and in the dating world. We giggled one night while out in a bar, single and rolling our eyes at the sad specimens of men. We tapped our glasses and toasted to ourselves. Living with her taught me to live for the moment, to laugh, enjoy and, in the process, to learn. We cooked, gardened, and usually broke the rules.

I took this playful wisdom and passed it down to my son Josh. As a baby, his second-floor bedroom had a vaulted ceiling and unfinished pine floors. I painted clouds on the ceiling, and when he became a toddler, we would lie on the floor and imagine what the clouds were. One was a dolphin, a dragon, an alligator. Funny, when I painted them, I had no intention of them looking like animals. I was just painting clouds. But it was the start of a great imagination.

As he got older, he decided the unfinished floor needed some paint. So, at 4 years old, he picked up a paint brush, and we painted the floor to look like a black and white racing checkered flag. I can still see his face, so proud. His second bedroom was in the condo I bought after the divorce. By then he was into skateboarding and biking. At age 7, he decided he wanted a giant wall with his name painted in graffiti letters and on his accent wall, black crackle paint. His creativity is on a roll and our home becomes more and more unique.

The next bedroom was the most fun. We had moved out to the beach, and his pre-teen bedroom was big and completely unfinished. He actually had two rooms: a work shop and a bedroom. One day when he had a friend over, he asked if he could take the wall down that separated the two. He had a vision, he said. It took some time, but when he was done, I walked in through the door that was now painted black with a skateboard logo and hinged from the opposite side so the door opened backwards. Colorful rope lights hung on the ceiling, silver tin roofing lined one wall, another wall was decorated with colorful blankets stapled to the walls. Another wall held a two-story bed structure with purple velvet movie curtains. The radio was on, and in the middle of the room--from wall to wall—was an 18-foot skateboard ramp made with 8-foot wood platforms. The sound of music was drowned out by the screech of his skateboard wheels back and forth, back and forth across the skateboard ramp.

It's just paint, I reminded myself. Paint and wood, lights, staples and nails. He will never forget these bedrooms, and when he's happy, I'm happy. He was learning to become his own unique person.

Life is so ironic.
It takes sadness to know what happiness is,
noise to appreciate silence,
and absence to value presence.
~Unknown

CHAPTER 20

Recharge Your Batteries

MY GRANDPARENTS MOVED TO WASHINGTON, New Hampshire when I was in high school. My son Josh remembers camp as "blueberry pie great Grammy." She taught him to climb trees, build teepees and paint his Indian war paint on with beet skins when she canned beets from the garden. He never got to meet his great grampy, but he recognized him in the pictures hanging on the wall and called him his "white-haired grampy."

When my batteries need recharging, I head to the cabin. This beautiful place was passed down from my grandparents to my parents and then to my husband and I.

Once you take a left up the dirt road, you can just feel the stress melt away. The fall brings you all the shades of yellow, orange, and red and the crisp cool air. The summer is filled with green grass, acres of flowers and sweet peas in the garden. Winter is magical: icy white snow and sparkling icicles dripping from the evergreens. The wood stove is warm and sizzles with bacon and fresh coffee brewing. Fall brings apple pies baking in the oven and chili on the stove. The cabin is made for lazy daytime napping, always a must. Writing is more inspired and hair sculptures are created with ease at the cabin.

A small 15 x 18 wooden structure with no insulation, a wood stove, some antique dishes and some mismatched comfy blankets. The cabin's walls hold the yard sale finds of antique metal perch coffee pots, the ceiling's filled with vintage baskets and one wall is lined with old books. The chalk board above the kitchen sink says, "you're at camp... RELAX!" And that's exactly what I do when I'm there. It's my escape, a slowdown, a breath of fresh air.

We have no running water but there's an old-fashioned red hand pump, an outhouse and the 4-glass fuse box boasts enough electricity to run a stove, the ceiling fan, a few lights and a toaster. I'm truly grateful it does have electricity. Although you can't run the toaster and the electric frying pan at once without blowing a fuse, I swear you can listen to your hair grow, the stars are brighter, and the cell signal is weak!

Whether I'm sitting at my computer banging out a few

chapters of the next New York times' best seller (at least that's what I'm hoping for) or gluing or braiding a hair sculpture for the next photo shoot (that could possibly grace the front cover of a national magazine), the cabin usually makes creativity come with ease. My grandmother and grandfather were both artists in their day. My grandmother, a more conventional artist with a flare in all categories, she spent her days cooking, gardening, braiding wool rugs, and collecting books. She was a librarian for many years and even published her own cookbook. My grandfather was a master potter. He belonged to the New Hampshire League of Craftsman and clay was his medium. My home is filled with his art, and on occasion, I can find a piece of his work on eBay. It's like a treasure hunt at times, searching yard sales and online sales to find his pieces. So, I guess that's part of the puzzle of where my creativity came from.

I fondly remember building elbow pots and eyeball mirrors of clay with my grandfather when I was a kid. My grandfather spoke softly and slowly like a wise old man. He had wispy feathers of white hair and his pure Irish skin was peppered with soft freckles. He would roll a piece of clay, roll up his sleeve and squish it around his elbow to form a bowl, then coil a small piece of clay and attach it to the bottom so this elbow bowl would stand up. Then he'd take another golf-ball-sized clay lump, show us how to sink our thumbs in and pinch the edges, then take a quarter size mirror and sink it inside the clay.

"A mirror for just your eyeball and a pot made from your elbow," he would say with a childish grin.

I have sat inside writing on cold snowy days in front of the wood stove, and on sunny days, I've sat under the apple tree with a mannequin set up, studying new braiding techniques. I've spent lazy snow storm days in my pj's napping and reading a book. The cabin is my little slice of creative heaven and I guard it zealously!

One day literally wrapped up in a memory under the warm off-white crotched afghan, I could hear in my mind Edie's voice is if she was next to me: *men are only good for three things... paying the bills, carrying the luggage and bringing in the Christmas tree.* My mind raced like a movie reel gone mad as I smiled and remembered my dear friend Edie. We met in my hair chair over 30 years ago. Every Tuesday morning at 10:30, she sat in my chair for her weekly shampoo and blowdry. I feel like it was yesterday, but she has been gone well over 10 years. I reached up and brushed the side of my face, and my fingers touched the gold earrings given to me by her daughter after Edie passed.

The cabin quieted my mind, and I lived in the moment, often recalling memories. This peaceful place lets me just sit in their light. I walked across the room to my grandmother's hope chest and lifted the cedar lid. It feels like I'm opening the secret door to a forgotten world. The lid creaks, and I can smell the fresh scent of cedar. That hope chest must be 80 years old and still holds its fresh scent. Handed down by my maternal grandmother, it came to me empty, her stories removed and an empty space for my stories to begin.

My first glance makes me smile as I see the faded yellow polka dot bikini. It moved with me from home to home for the last 30 years, tucked away safe in that cedar chest. The elastic has almost disintegrated, but the memories are clear. I once wanted to shadow box it and hang it on the wall to prove that, YES, I did wear that AND won a bikini contest!

I can feel that Cancun wind, I can taste the tequila and hear the party around me. Me in my yellow polka dot bikini.

Edie was in her late 60's at the time and a weekly client with enough hairspray to withstand hurricane force winds. Every Valentine's Day she would let her husband carry her bags to the car and off she went with her girlfriends to Cancun for the week. They shot tequila and were the life of the party at the island resort.

Edie, 30 years older than me, raved about the place in Cancun and persuaded my husband and me to go on vacation there. "Enter the bikini contest when your there," Edie said.

"They don't tell you what the prize is, but it's a week's stay back at the resort."

I chuckled and said, "Sure, I'll remember."

You should have seen her smiling face as she sat in the hair chair the following Tuesday morning at 10:30, and I shared the story of the little yellow polka dot bikini! Her eyes lit up with a sparkle and she clapped her hands!

Edie's best advice for a successful marriage was always let him think he's right!" Every week on Tuesday at 10:30, I would drape my magic cape over Edie shoulders and wash, blow-dry and spray (Edie used enough finishing spray to create a helmet), she would say, "I feel a soft spot?" and ask for more finishing spray to make her hair last all week. Chilled Champagne was her favorite nail polish, and she wore it every day for the last 20 years. I'd always joke as she got older that someday I would paint her nails red! She said, "Not a chance, no way!"

When she became sick with COPD, I would travel to her home every week to make her beautiful and hairspray a helmet-strength coating for her to last another week. We talked about cheap vodka vs expensive stuff you saved for special occasions. We laughed about adult diapers and about how her TV show was at a pivotal moment, when she decided to test out the strength of them!

"Oh no you didn't," I said.

She laughed. "Oh yes, I did."

I sat in Intensive Care holding her hand the night before

she died, and I had that red nail polish in my pocket. She died on Valentine's Day, finally reunited with Bob, her beloved husband.

From the hair chair to a yellow polka dot bikini, I adopted a longtime friend. I keep the blanket her son gave me after she passed away safe in the hope chest of dreams and memories.

I am sentimental. So much so that my son's girlfriend recently spent a night at our cabin and said, "I feel like I'm in an old museum filled with memories."

My sentimental soul wants to travel back in time, bake a blueberry pie with Grammy, watch my grandfather throw one more pot on his pottery wheel, and listen to his deep soft voice telling me how easy it is to magically construct a two feet tall masterpiece. I want to drink expensive vodka with Edie and just thinking of her reminds me to take time while the others are still here. I want to pick up sticks with my dad for the campfire, get up early and have coffee with mom, spend more time with my son, stay late for a client, be compassionate to my coworkers, and spend more time with friends making memories.

My clients know the cabin is my escape; my trade show crew knows the cabin gives me the peace I need to create amazing hair sculpture; my mom and dad know the cabin is a slowdown; my son, my coworkers, and my friends know it's a place for me to shut down, reflect, recharge and create. And I see it as the most magical cozy warmest place in the world.

Taking time to do nothing
often brings everything into perspective.
~Unknown

CHAPTER 21

Aahhh...

WHEN I'M on the motorcycle and the wind blows through my hair, life feels so much clearer. My thoughts are wild but flow freely. I realize that most of my life I have mastered multi-tasking 24/7, not slowing down often, but I am now learning to slow down a bit. When I ride I can do only two things, drive and think. I think about life, I think about how you spend a good portion of your life finding your way, I think about building your dreams and about how when you get to the top of the mountain of life, you reflect.

The last three years have been years of reflection. Turning fifty, the aches, pains, and fatigue of menopause, and the question that arises is maybe menopause is "life" telling us to slow down? It physically tries to disable you and mentally throws you a curve ball.

The last three years have seemed like a snowstorm of life whirling around in a glass snow globe. The snowflakes are settling, and the scene is serene, beautiful, and peaceful. I call it #theothersideoffifty. I've started to build my personalized life survival kit, one that keeps me happy, healthy and inspired. I have an amazing husband, a loving son. My heart is filled with love for family and gratitude for friends.

As the cool fall air whisks past my face, I take a deep breath and exhale, my shoulders drop a little, more relaxed, and I grab another gear. Riding is a freedom. I have a t-shirt that says, "You never see a motorcycle outside a therapist's office." Riding my motorcycle is one form of therapy. I am at peace. I pull over to watch the sunset, put the kick stand down, and turn off the rumble of the Harley. Sunsets and sunrise are my peace, another therapy. I take a walk to the water's edge and look back at my license plate *aahhh*, I smile.

These are the times I can quiet my mind.

I've driven the loop around the lake that my brother took to clear his head, the place my friend Michelle sits to take a breath, the place I sat with my ex-husband and had our only civil conversation about our marriage being over. Now I sit by the edge of this water and reflect.

Water is where my dream started. The Water's Edge Salon and Spa opened on the shores of Beaver Brook in

Windham, New Hampshire, Mother's Day weekend 1990. Where did the last 30 years go? What a ride!

I reflect back to a time that success meant money. My first motorcycle was the first time I bought myself a prize. After eating mac and cheese, almost going bankrupt, and getting a divorce, my accountant said to me, "Go buy a Harley. You deserve it." She knew it was a dream I thought may never come true. It was like a benchmark of success. But actual money wasn't my motivator. The feeling of happiness, passion and excitement was always the engine that drove me.

I have been lucky. I've been in a profession I have loved since I was young, and it still excites me, though my dreams have shifted. My dreams haven't changed, just shifted and like an Olympic event, I am passing the baton to Sheri, my business partner and friend. I have found someone with the drive to make the world a better place, to inspire people, to run a team of talented professionals and to continue the legacy of the Water's Edge.

Sheri and I have been the Thelma and Louise of the business world, working hard and playing hard for the past twenty years. We have been an unstoppable team, building a business, a team and a culture. I have chosen to live life half full. I have built a career and mastered a craft. My work is second nature and comes with ease. My hands may be crooked and I may need an Aleve for inflammation, but the passion for my career still burns bright, whether I'm standing behind the chair or on a stage inspiring others, it's my happy place. The other side of fifty for me is living for the moment, doing what's right for me and with no regrets. Not plowing over people to get what I want, just being honest about what I want.

I took a look in the mirror and my reflection was at peace. I almost dare to say I look younger. My lines of wisdom were softened. I no longer felt sweaty and defeated like a hamster on a wheel. Yes, I can truly say I am at peace. There is so much more out there, and it is time to pass the baton. I am grateful to have a successor who will continue to grow the legacy of Water's Edge Salon and Spa.

One day at a time to the fullest. I see my dreams shift. As I hand the key to the castle to Sheri, I look over my shoulder with immense pride...*Friend, I'm always back stage if you need me.*

Enjoy the Journey
As the journey continues, As the Chair Turns, book 2 coming soon! ...Because book one wasn't enough time to tell 50 plus years of stories I have logged in my heart.

ABOUT THE AUTHOR

Shelly Devlin is an artist at heart.

Her business card boasts "Inspyr-a-tional Coach" and she is a hairdresser extraordinaire for longer than some of you have been alive.

A Salon owner of The Water's Edge Salon and Spa for over a quarter of a century and her hair art has been published numerous times in Modern Salon, Hot and Canadian Hairdresser magazine to name a few.

She has held the Mrs. NH 1999 title and competed for the Mrs. America title when she fit into a size six dress.

She is a grateful Daughter to her biggest fans, her mom and dad.

She is a Mother of an extremely talented son and a Wife to an amazing husband she swears is from another planet. Shelly and her husband Josh live on a quiet lake with their two dogs .

If she is not writing or making people beautiful...She enjoys slowing down as the wind blows through her hair while riding her Harley with a license plate AAHHH!

Explore the world behind the scenes of *As the Chair Turns* go to ShellyDevlin.life and sneak a peak of the magical cabin, The Waters Edge Salon and more of Shellys adventures

facebook.com/shellydevlininspyr

twitter.com/shelly_devlin

instagram.com/shellydevlin

Made in the USA
Middletown, DE
20 September 2020